Abel

The punishment list

A collection of spanking stories

The punishment list
Abel

First published in Great Britain in 2010 by
Abelard Books
www.abelardbooks.co.uk

Text © Abel 2010
Cover art © Catherine Thomas 2010

To my darling wife Haron, with love

A catalogue record for this book is available from the British Library

ISBN 978-0-9558483-2-2

The moral rights of the author have been asserted. All rights reserved. No part of this publication may be reproduced, stored in a retrieval system or transmitted in any form or by any means, electronic, mechanical or otherwise without the written permission of the Publisher.

With thanks to Catherine for the wonderful front cover; to Martha for the painstaking proofreading, and to Alison for her additional support – as well as to Haron for her help with design and technical issues.

The punishment list

1.	Anna and the headmaster	p. 5
2.	A maid of two masters	p. 14
3.	Sanctuary lost	p. 26
4.	The girl behind the counter	p. 34
5.	The punishment list	p. 37
6.	The occupation	p. 57
7.	The green slip	p. 64
8.	Five stars, six stripes	p. 71
9.	Twenty four of the best	p. 81
10.	The punishment cell	p. 98
11.	The housemaster's secret diary	p. 100
12.	From left to right	p. 110
13.	The sequence of events	p. 116
14.	The colonials	p. 122
15.	The punishment dorm	p. 134
16.	Middlington	p. 154
17.	The price of privilege	p. 171
18.	Someone to care	p. 184

Anna and the headmaster

She'd been the first girl in her year at Willingdon to be caned. The school rulebook that they'd each been sent – and had had to memorise – before their arrival had been manifestly clear on the role that corporal punishment played in the school's disciplinary regime. The headmaster's inaugural lecture, welcoming them to the establishment, had removed any lingering doubt that could possibly have remained.

Iris Palmer - a giggly, friendly, immensely-likeable girl in the next dorm - had actually been the first to find herself called to the headmaster's study. Her fellow new starters waited with baited breath to learn of the outcome: she later confessed that she almost felt as though she'd let them down when she had returned after a strict lecture ("he made me feel as if I was, so, like, *twelve*") and with a dire final warning ("if I find you before me again, you can be sure that I shall be cognisant of the fact that you have taken advantage of my leniency").

Her own call had been two days later, at the end of the school day, and this time the waiting audience would find itself disappointed only by their friend's taciturn reluctance to describe the painful ceremony for their enlightenment and entertainment. She could still remember the chill of the moment when her housemaster had told her that a mere detention would not suffice for behaviour of this most disappointing nature, especially from someone so new to Willingdon.

He'd reached into his drawer and taken out a leather folder, from which he'd extracted a pink sheet of paper. As he wrote, his traditional fountain pen filling the page with scrawling blue ink, he'd explained what he was doing: noting details of her offence, so that she could take it to the headmaster for him to deal with her. No specific mention of the cane. No room for confusion left as to its inevitability.

Heart pounding, she'd crossed the quad towards the headmaster's house. "The front door will be unlocked"; her hands were shaking as she pushed it open. "You'll find his secretary's office on the right hand side"; her tongue scarcely co-operated as she mumbled the reason for her visit.

She was shown to a waiting room, comfortably furnished: trophies filling the cabinets, the walls crammed with photographs from glorious schooldays gone by. This would be where her mother and father had sat, she presumed, before being interviewed by the headmaster as the final stage of the school's exacting selection process, once she herself had already passed the admission exam with flying colours. They'd have sat together. She sat alone, trying to banish all thought of her parents, and how disappointed and ashamed they'd be, were they to know of their only child's current predicament.

A grandfather clock in the corner ticked away the minutes. One, two, five, ten, before the front door swung open once more and a flurry of black gown and books and papers breezed past, and she heard a heavy door being opened and closed. Within moments, the headmaster's secretary was before her in the doorway. Her voice tried to reassure, but her message did not: "He is free to see you now," pointing the new girl along the corridor to the door at the far end. "Knock before entering, and wait until he calls you."

Stephenson was kinder than she'd feared. "You must be Anna." He rose to meet her: shook her hand, to introduce himself. "I remember you doing remarkably well in our entrance tests; I'm delighted you could join us. But I hear that a little issue has arisen?"

A *little* issue? If only that were true. As crimes go, it can't have been the worst ever, but it had been deemed grave enough to bring her here. "Yes, sir. I'm sorry to trouble you, sir," as if good manners might cause him to spare her. She handed over the pink punishment form.

He reached for his spectacles, and studied the details intently. "I see..." Saw that she had argued with Mrs Cooper when she'd been awarded the detention; saw that she'd failed to attend the following evening when instructed to do so; read how she'd again been absent from the detention room the next day, despite the cautionary note from her housemaster.

The headmaster took a small fob of keys from his desk drawer, and walked across to open a tall cupboard in the corner of the room. He continued the conversation as he did so: "Most regrettable. Girls must learn to respect authority here at Willingdon, even if we don't always expect them to *agree* with every decision." He picked out a cane, the last vestige of doubt now in smithereens. "And on this occasion you seem to have ignored a very clear warning from your housemaster, who had been so kind as to give you a second chance. Most disappointing."

She would have liked to argue; she knew his words rang true. Why had she been so foolish, she wondered, wishing - like almost every girl rooted to this daunting spot in these circumstances - that she could turn back time.

"I am absolutely sure that you are a good girl, Anna, who is going to do extremely well with us here. And I look forward to celebrating your successes with you over the years. But I'm afraid that in such circumstances I have no choice other than to give you three strokes of the cane."

"I'm so sorry, sir." Apologising to him helped her stop feeling sorry for herself.

"As am I." He'd walked to her side now, and touched a point on the floor in front of her with the cane. "Please bend forward and touch the carpet here with your fingertips."

He moved behind her. She stretched down. The moment was here.

Reflecting in later months, she realised that his strokes – her strokes - were administered with great leniency. At the time, it felt like the most painful experience imaginable, each searing line demonstrating the school's disapproval in the most agonising way.

And then it was over, and he was walking away from her to hang up the cane. Over his shoulder, he asked her to stand. "I'm sorry to have had to do that, Anna, and I'm sure that I won't have to repeat myself in future with one so bright."

He asked her to let herself out, her hands shaking just as badly as she turned the door handle as they had done on her arrival, only this time with her vision blurred by tears. She rubbed her burning backside as she walked back along the corridor, stepping into the cool outside air and praying for somewhere to hide.

--

He did have to repeat himself, of course, just two weeks later, only this time he introduced her to the agonies of a full-force six of the best. Once again, she acknowledged to herself, the punishment was both fair and deserved, breaching a golden rule so clearly laid out in the school regulations. Once again, she asked herself why she had been so idiotic. She'd never even smoked before; she swore that she never would again.

This time, the cane was out on his desk before they even arrived.

That Danielle – Dannie, her new best buddy – had accompanied her to be punished at the same time made the whole process even more painful. Anna found herself cast into the role of reluctant expert as they acted out the familiar opening scenes: hand-holder, reassurer, comforter, when she so needed reassuring and comforting herself.

They were sent down that long, dark, dreaded corridor together. Lectured on the perils of tobacco, as every girl caught smoking in every school had been lectured in the past, and told that they would be caned, as had each of their predecessors.

He asked Anna to stand to the side and watch "so that you may learn something from your friend's experience as well as your own". The headmaster explained the punishment position to Dannie; her best friend looked on aghast.

Which of the two girls gave the louder sob as the first stroke descended would have been hard to tell – Dannie at the shock of the impact, Anna at its sight. By the sixth, there would be no doubt, as the punished girl sobbed her apologies. As the spectator prayed for the punishment to be over quickly, for her friend's sake, she prayed too for it to never end, for her own.

The two girls didn't speak to each other as they swapped positions; couldn't even bring themselves to make eye contact.

Anna took her place, the very touch of that carpet confirming the immediacy of her plight. It was then, and only then, that Stephenson informed how let down he felt - how *very* disappointed; how he intended to nip this emerging pattern of disrespect for Willingdon's rules and culture in the bud once and for all.

Two girls caned in succession can never be sure whether one has taken whacks more fearsome than the other: the perspectives of punishee and audience are too different to permit fair comparisons, and the done thing is always to sympathise that the other "took it so much harder". Yet Anna's observation had suggested that Dannie's strokes had looked comparable to her own first experience; later, her friend's marks and her own weals would illustrate his determination to make this second lesson count.

My goodness, the first batch of strokes had hurt. But this time, the rod lifted higher, descended more vigorously, as the headmaster cracked home his disapproval more painfully than she could have imagined possible.

She leapt to her feet after the second; the pain was quite unbearable. "I shall let that count on this occasion," she heard a distant voice pledge, "but I shall not be so generous if you fail to take any of the remaining four properly." And strangely, it was the desire not to seem ungrateful for his generosity, not to let him down still further, that bound her into place as the third, the awful fourth, the fifth, the quite astonishing sixth laid their agonising stripes.

--

He didn't so much *expel* her on her third and final visit to his study, a week before the Christmas holiday, as *suggest* to her parents – who had driven up from Devon for the appointment, and who now sat beside her in shock – that "Anna might be happier were she able to make a fresh start somewhere else."

"She's a bright girl, of that I have no doubt. Her results in last week's end-of-term examinations were absolutely excellent. However, she seems to have had problems adjusting to our disciplinary regime, and this latest incident" – a fearsome argument with Mr White, the Chemistry teacher, which she'd brought to an end with an obscene phrase quite unacceptable from pupil to schoolmaster – "really does seem to be the final straw."

Her mother, sitting next to her on the leather couch, tried valiantly to intervene: "I'm sure she didn't mean it. Anna's not like that, you see. She's always been brought up to be a well-behaved girl." For good measure, her father weighed in: "And she was never in trouble at her previous school; they even appointed her as a monitor in her final year."

Bombshells rarely remain secret; she'd prayed that he wouldn't, but the headmaster dropped his. "Mr and Mrs Montague, I have already had to cane Anna twice this term." Their shocked eyes turned to hers; she buried her face in her hands. "Most girls enjoy their time with us here without experiencing corporal punishment at all. This will be Anna's third taste of the cane…"

… hold on…

… third?…

… you mean he's not just going to send me away…

… the cane…

… noooooooooo…

… he can't…

… but my parents are here…

… pleeeeeaaaasssse…

Stephenson was speaking again. "…and frankly I've never previously had a girl reappear to be disciplined for a third time in the same term." He looked up at them. "I understand that this might be a shock to you, and please accept my assurance that I don't take decisions like this at all lightly."

"Do you really have to cane her? Can't we just take her home?" Her father spoke up, counsel for the defence, although he already knew the answer.

"I'm sure you wouldn't wish to question my judgement, Mr Montague." It was a statement, not a question.

"Of course not..." Her father's voice trailed off, and with it her final hopes.

"On a brighter note, I have taken the liberty on your behalf of calling a good friend of mine, Gerald Goodson, who's headmaster at Norling Hall. A wonderful school. You might know it?"

The family nodded, in unison. It had been their other choice for Anna: she'd sailed through the entrance exam there, too, and it was only the memory that Mrs Montague's cousin had been so happy at Willingdon that had swung the balance in its favour.

"Frankly, though it pains me to say it, they beat us in last year's A Level results – and, as a small favour to me, Mr Goodson has kindly indicated his willingness to allow Anna to transfer over from the start of next term."

Her parents were, if not delighted, then incredibly relieved; Anna was immediately desolate. She *liked* Willingdon. This was her world now. Her friends were here. She couldn't bear to have to say goodbye to them. Couldn't face being the new girl thrown into the midst of a crowd of strangers who'd already been together for months.

"Now, Mr and Mrs Montague, if you could perhaps retire to the sitting room, I need to have a final little..." – he hesitated, as if lost for words – "...little *discussion* with Anna. And then perhaps she might take you up to her dormitory to pack her things, and it might be rather a good idea if she travelled home with you this afternoon, don't you think?"

--

And then they were alone. Silent for a few moments. His subsequent message had been clear: that he liked her, knew she meant well, knew she wanted to succeed. That *he* wanted her to succeed and had confidence in her; that she would thrive at Norling Hall.

That he intended to give her a final clear reminder of the importance of good behaviour, lest she be tempted to stray down the wrong path again in the new year.

That he also intended to punish her most severely for her foul language towards Mr White.

He would be using the senior cane this time, he explained. He really wanted this caning to succeed, where its predecessors had clearly failed. And that she might find it easier to bend over his desk, and to hold tight onto the far edge...

"... for six strokes, once more. Only this time on the bare. Shall we get this over with?"

Terrified, she clambered to her feet, walked towards his desk, lifted her skirt and leant forward. At the last moment, she reached back to slide down her knickers before stretching forward, taut, grasping the opposite side.

Then, yet again, he surpassed his previous efforts – the swing could scarcely have been higher, the power of the strokes could scarcely have been harder, but the extra weight of the oh-so-dense, oh-so-whippy rattan administered without the scant protection of her uniform cracked into her as though the previous cane had been a feather.

Only this time, she managed not to cry – to show her soon-to-be-ex-headmaster that Anna Montague was a brave girl. (The sobbing would come later, much later, in her bedroom at home that night, when she was finally oh-so-alone after her long, uncomfortable and silent journey).

Afterwards, Stephenson gave her a hug. "You owe it to yourself to do well, Anna," he said. She vowed that she would; he *knew* that she would - and she closed his office door behind her for the final time, to face her future.

--

The new headmaster gathered his prefects together on the opening day of the autumn term, as his predecessor had always done. Moving to a new school was a fascinating challenge – and his smile suggested that he was relishing the role.

He started by congratulating the girls once again on their selection, as so many others had congratulated them since their appointments had been announced by the departing head at the final assembly that had closed the previous school year.

He thanked them for the work they were to undertake; explained the incomparable importance of the role the prefects played in keeping a school happy and successful. He wished them well. A carefully-prepared homily: one that had served him well over the years at his former establishment.

Here, though, to his surprise, the head girl rose to her feet once he had finished speaking. "And on behalf of the prefects, might I be so impertinent – but with the best possible intent – as to say in return that we too wish *you* every happiness as our new headmaster? We all loved Mr Goodson very dearly, and he will be sorely missed. But we have no doubt that you will be a quite wonderful successor, Mr Stephenson, here at Norling Hall."

And then there was work to be done – a new school year ahead, with all of its impending triumphs and inevitable minor disasters. He sent the prefectorial elite on their way – but asked his head girl to stay behind for a moment.

After the others had shut the door behind them, he gave her another hug, before telling Anna Montague quite how delighted and proud he was to see the way in which she had so evidently flourished in the past few years since their previous meeting.

She smiled back at her new, old headmaster: "And if there's anything at all I can do to help you to settle in, sir, I'd be delighted. After all, I know the first term can sometimes be a little tricky…"

A maid of two masters

The list, in the butler's scrawling handwriting. Still there, pinned to the wall, on the ever-so-neat Lindsham House notepaper.

She placed the silver tray down carefully on the scullery table, and sneaked another glance. Perhaps she was dreaming? Perhaps his was a magical writing – the name that appeared being an illusion, to scare her, only to be replaced by the guest's true identity on the fourth, the fifth look.

If it was an illusion, it was one that was persisting for far too long.

--

The sharp stones on the driveway cutting her bruised feet as she walked towards the big house in her worn-through shoes... The cool, damp touch of the grass as she stepped aside suddenly to let the rider gallop past on the big black horse: a blur of pace and animal and fine cloth and steam.

Watching the finely-clad gentleman dismounting elegantly in front of the mansion, two servants rushing immediately to his aid. The third member of staff racing towards her, purple-faced, waving one of his master's riding whips like a scimitar.

Shouting: inaudible at first. Inaudibly inhospitable. The phrases sharpening as he drew nearer: "Clear off at once. Be gone! This is private property, do you hear me?"

"But sir, I just..."

The force of the crop across her arm as she raised it to defend herself from his blow. Shock, numbness, giving way to the pain. "Private property, I tell you."

Shouts in their direction from the big house. Eyes welling with tears, but able to see the gentleman striding towards them.

"Leave it to me, Watkins."

"Yes, sir." The purple-faced servant retreated, throwing her a glare of hatred and contempt as he exited the scene.

What to do? Faced with a real gentleman like this?

She fell to her knees on the grass.

And he laughed, not unkindly. "I sometimes get curtseys, but rarely do young ladies feel the need to fall to the ground before me." He stretched out a hand and lifted her up. "So what brings such a pretty yet bedraggled girl up my driveway this spring morning?"

What indeed? To tell of her father – losing his job, losing his temper...? To tell of her hopes? To ask for food: any food, even the scraps, after four long days on the road, after last night in the inn, fleeing with her meal still on the table as the group of men had drawn closer around her.

"I was hoping you might have a job for an honest girl, sir."

Honest. That much was true. Kind, bright. Hard-working.

Scared.

And he did, of course, like some fairytale benefactor. Nothing much – she had no skills, after all, other than the sewing that she'd learned at Sunday School and the cooking she'd picked up after her mother had lost interest. Not that their meagre diet compared one jot to the fabulous feasts she grew to love at Delaware Hall. Love as a spectator, sniffing the air as the dishes went past. Love, eventually, as a part of the show itself, promoted to wait on tables before the lords and ladies as she proved herself to be competent, good natured, trustworthy.

She had to be. She had to repay her master for his generosity. She couldn't betray him, after all he'd done. His

Lordship was renowned for remaining somewhat aloof from the servants, but at the sight of her the corners of his mouth seemed to twitch invariably into a smile in the midst of even the most distinguished gatherings. He was the one who'd rescued her, after all – not that that endeared her to the purple-faced butler, who often as not would round off an evening's service by cuffing her round the ear for over-familiarity.

And at least it was only cuffs. She'd quickly understood that it was better to cover her ears when the other girls lay crying after Mr Watkins had administered one of his none-too-irregular thrashings. To creep under the pillow, to keep one's head down, to stay out of his sight and out of his reach.

--

At least she hadn't been allocated to look after *his* room. She was taking care of Sir George Sanderson, together with his wife.

Wife. Yes, that's what she was. Some of the staff were gossiping, of course – the lady seemed somewhat younger than might have been expected, somewhat prettier. One claimed to have seen a portrait once of Sir George with a dark-haired lady at his side, and this companion was fair. It was even said that she had looked taken aback the first time she was addressed as Lady Sanderson. But Sir George's 'wife'. Of course.

Tidy their room, keep it clean, make sure their garments were laid out on time.

No need to see *him*. No need at all. Even if the magic had not yet worked its tricks, and his Lordship's name did still appear on the notice.

--

"You look as if you've just seen a ghost, Becky!"

That ghost of times past, across the hallway as she was carrying a tray to Sir George and his lady. A ghost all too solid in form, talking to her new master, the two of them fresh back from a bracing early morning walk across the estate.

That ghost, who haunted her sleepless nights to this day.

"It's nothing. I just felt a little faint. I'll be fine."

--

"You look as if you've just seen a ghost, Edward."
   "How very strange."
   "Now my dear friend, what are you talking about?"
   "That girl. Where did you get her?"
   "Which girl?"
   "The one who just walked past carrying a breakfast tray."
   "And how would I know that?" Sir James looked almost offended. "I don't especially make a habit of getting involved in staff maters, you know. Anyway, why do you ask?"

--

It was the second handwritten note on the board that stopped her breath: "Would any girl previously in the employ of Lord Edward Delaware please inform me forthwith, and no later than the start of dinner this evening."
   Had he recognised her? Surely not. He'd been facing the other way. He'd been talking to Sir James, not gazing at the servants. She was older now: only a year, but she must look different. Her hair was cut short. She'd lost a little weight. The uniform was different.
   Luncheon came and went.
   She had no need to identify herself. There was no paperwork: nothing to identify her.
   An afternoon spent deep in the bowels of the house, folding sheets, folding napkins, re-folding, re-ordering the piles, safe in the darkness of the dimmest of cupboards.
   Afternoon tea. Served on the lawn, in the fine weather. Not by her: Sir George's bed was rather crumpled, and needed remaking.
   Silverware to polish, too much to let her stray upstairs. And then the butler appeared. "A busy day, Becky."
   "Yes, Mr Thompson."
   "I'd like you to wait on table at dinner this evening."

But... He'd be... And... "I'm feeling a little unwell, sir. I'm not sure that would be wise. I wouldn't want to make any of the guests ill."

He took her face roughly in his calloused hand, twisting it, glaring into her eyes. "Look fine to me, girl. Remember: best manners all night. This is an important weekend for our master. Sir James has told me that only excellence will suffice. I know I can rely on you."

--

Of course he recognised her. How couldn't he? He was an intelligent man: good with facts, good with figures and, it seemed, good with faces.

He placed his hand on her arm, as she tried to step back after serving the potatoes. "I told you, Sir James. Becky, if I remember correctly."

Her new master looked at her. "Becky?"

She averted her eyes. "Yes, sir."

Now it was just a matter of whether he would say anything.

"She worked for me at Delaware Hall." But like a true gentleman, not wishing to disturb the flow of an excellent dinner, his Lordship saved the remainder of the story for a whispered conversation with Sir James later in the evening, next to the fireplace, over their glasses of port.

--

It had been another dinner, if anything even more formal – not surprising, given the kudos associated with hosting their guest of honour at Delaware Hall. Prince Aleksander of Prussia. A tall, intense, serious, deeply dislikeable man – one born to privilege, to expect the very finest, and to scarcely notice when it was laid before him.

Everything imaginable had been done to pamper the Prince. The finest wines had been dug out of his Lordship's cellars, the freshest salmon brought twitching from the stream to the kitchens, the best stag on the estate persuaded to walk across the line of fire just as the Prince had raised his gun during the hunt.

Becky had been serving the wine: a red, she recalled, with French writing on the label. He must have been on his third, fourth glass. She'd leant forward to refill his crystal; he'd nudged her arm as she did. The wine missed him – thank goodness – but splattered the table.

"You should take care," he bellowed.

"I was trying my hardest, sir," she replied.

And then the table fell silent.

Silent.

Silent.

Silent.

Every eye was looking at them.

The Prince turned to his Lordship. "I cannot recall being spoken to with such insolence by a servant girl."

Her master looked pale. "Your Highness, I can only apologise. Butler – relieve the girl of her duties immediately."

The Prince protested immediately: "And that is *it*?"

"Your Highness?"

"A girl who spoke like that in my palace would surely be flogged until she learned to hold her tongue."

"I am sure the butler will discuss her conduct with her, Your Highness."

"In Prussia, a true gentleman would avenge a grave insult personally, not pass responsibility to his staff to 'discuss'."

Silence.

Silence.

"Then you may rest assured that I shall indeed punish the girl myself. But might I suggest that we leave that to the morning, and enjoy the rest of this evening's festivities."

"But of course." The Prince raised his half-empty glass: "To justice."

"To justice!"

Becky fled to her bed, of course, inconsolable. What would happen to her? Surely her master would not... could not... He'd know she'd not meant to sound insolent. He'd leave it to morning until the Prince, placated by the splendour of the previous evening's meal, would be calmer; he'd have a quiet word; explain how things were done in England.

An hour, more, must have passed by the time the butler appeared at her bedside. No friend, he: the manner of her original arrival meant that the Prince was not the only one keen to see her brought down.

She stood, brushed down her dress, awaited his news.

"His Lordship will see you in his study after breakfast tomorrow morning."

"Yes, Mr Watkins. Is he very angry with me?"

"That is for him to tell you, girl. But you should know that he has asked me to take a walk into the forest at dawn and to cut him a selection of the finest birches."

--

It'd been dark when she had left. A dry night, thank goodness, the clear sky illuminating her route back down that driveway that had led her first to peace, safety, security. And was now leading her to... Who knew?

Where would she go?

She'd saved the shillings from her weekly wage pack: for when she was married, perhaps – for that knight must surely gallop over the hill for her one day?

If she walked back towards the town ... Maybe she could find a stagecoach?

And so it was that she had come to Lindsham, tired but telling tale of her experience and her aptitude for hard work. Her newly-minted reference had helped, of course - courtesy of an ever-so-neat writer at the inn she had slept in on the second night, and the pile of notepaper she had grabbed from the butler's room as she had made her escape.

--

The butler was up early at Lindsham the next morning; he was brushing mud from his boots as Becky appeared in the kitchens, fresh from the most sleepless of nights.

"Sir James will see you in his study after breakfast this morning."

"Mr Thompson?" This was not a good sign – for a maid to be called to see her master... If the butler knew any more, he had been sworn to silence. "Is he angry with me?" How much does he know?

--

What if a year ago, she'd had the nerve to stand before a different door, to a different study? She steadied herself outside this one, and raised her hand to knock. Then, her fate had been inevitable. Now, there was still the shadow of doubt, the glimmer of optimism.

Or there was, until she stepped inside, and found both masters, past and present, standing before her.

Lord Delaware, her former master broke the silence. "It would seem as though we have some unfinished business to deal with, young lady."

"Siiiiiiirrrrrrr..."

"I gave my word to the Prince that I would flog you, and I am a man of my word. It has merely taken rather longer to administer the punishment than he and I had perhaps anticipated."

"You can't...."

Sir James, her new master, intervened. "His Lordship can, and his Lordship will." He reached behind him to a desk, and passed over a fearsome bundle of rods. "Thompson appears to have been most professional in his preparations."

"Bend over." Lord Delaware took the birches, and pointed the girl to the arm of a leather chair. "And lift your skirt out of the way as you do, of course."

No "Nice to see you again." No "How are you?" No standing on ceremony. No time to argue. No room for debate. Trembling, she arranged herself in position.

Could it be all that bad?

The cold leather against her bare thighs.

It couldn't hurt that much.

The rods measured, precisely, across her bare buttocks.

She'd survive.

"I'd planned on giving you a dozen strokes last year. You may be well advised to take hold of the opposite arm of the chair, and to hold tight."

It would be over soon...

And then. Then, oh then, the moment she had fled and feared, and the imprint of the birch told her why. A pain worse than her nightmares had foretold, cutting and searing and burning.

And then again... Another, quite as hard, magnifying the agony.

Surely that would be it? The pain, unimaginable, unbearable, could get no worse?

And then... She howled, her composure quite gone, begging for mercy, pleading for forgiveness...

And then... Then she quite lost count. Longing for the strokes to be over, dreading lest they fell, knowing that they would. Praying that the force of the blows might ease, but her prayers going unanswered.

And then... A longer pause, her sobs filling empty air: a glance backwards; her punisher walking away.

"Stand up, face me." Lord Delaware's face was surprisingly sympathetic – a glimmer of the compassion he had shown her on his driveway that first morning, perhaps?

He continued, "I promised Prince Aleksander that you would be flogged. And I can now look him in the eye when we next meet."

"Yes, sir."

"Twelve months ago, young lady, you would have been standing before me in similar discomfort, flogged and sorry."

"Yes, sir. I am sorry, really I am."

He paused, and walked over to Sir James's desk. "And then you took it upon yourself to flee my house, quite in breach of your terms of employment, whilst stealing one of my uniforms, and taking – as I now understand it – a quantity of my butler's headed notepaper."

To her horror, she saw him pick up a fresh birch.

"And you must expect, young lady, that as a result you will be chastised more severely than you would have been were your insolence to His Royal Highness to be the only matter on our agenda."

"You can't...." Becky turned, ran towards the door, grabbed the handle.

"A wasted effort, young lady," explained Sir James calmly. "Your taste for flight in the face of adversity has already been noticed. Mr Thompson therefore took the precaution of locking the door behind you as you entered, and is waiting outside lest we need his assistance. Now, my Lord," as he turned to his friend, "I believe you were minded to administer a further dozen?"

Delaware pointed back to the chair. Becky realised that she had no choice.

No choice but to bare herself again, No choice but to bend back over the hateful leather arm, to reach out to steady herself. No choice but to scream from the very first blow, her unlucky thirteenth of a birch that (impossibly) felt even thicker than its predecessor. A thirteenth to be followed in quick succession by the fourteenth, fifteenth, more....

She tried counting this time, as if the effort of concentration would somehow occupy her entire body, distract it from the blows that were striping her backside, the tops of her thighs.

On twenty-two, it stopped. Had she miscounted? Was it over? Was he teasing her, provoking her, making her wait?

"It appears that your butler needs to study the art of birch-making some more, Sir James."

"Indeed. Stand up, girl."

She stood, turned around, clasping her behind, as if a few gentle rubs could soothe away the fires. Lord Delaware held out the birch – or what was left of it; it was obvious that the rods had disintegrated across her as they fell.

Now it was Sir James who spoke. "So you have made good your debt to his Lordship. And yet we are left with the undeniable fact that you are under my roof under false pretences, are we not?"

"Sir James?"

He picked up a sheet of paper from his desk, and turned to his friend. "Lord Delaware, do you recognise the writing on this letter?"

"I do not, Sir James."

"And would you recognise your butler's handwriting, my Lord?

"Of course, Sir James.

"Then I can only conclude that the young lady before us presented my staff with falsified references on her arrival here last year." He turned back to her: "Is that the case?"

She gulped. "Yes, sir."

"Then you will agree that you have committed a most serious offence?"

"Siiiiiiir..."

"Your choice, my girl. I can deal with it here, or we can send for the constable. I do warn you that the House of Correction is not an attractive place, mind, and a private whipping there would far outweigh anything you may have experienced here.

"Please, sir..."

"Your choice..."

And so it was that Becky found herself, quite naked ("You no longer have the right to wear my uniform"), legs apart, bent forward over her second master's oak desk.

"We use the rattan for discipline here; our supplies of birch are too limited," Sir James explained as he measured the single, whippy stick across her.

A single stick, maybe, but one which was to prove a worthy rival for the birch rods. Cutting deeper: pushing through the pain of her previous floggings to punish her more deeply than she could have dreamt possible.

He hadn't offered up a suggested number of strokes. She didn't count. Couldn't count – the caning took up all her emotions, left no room for logic. When Clara tried to trace the lines later, she guessed at fifteen, but who could tell?

And then she was standing before them, covering herself, as Sir James explained that her continued presence at Lindsham was quite inconceivable, and that Thompson would help her pack her things – and only *her* things, mind – ready to depart.

"But, nonetheless, she has been a good girl, aside from these few days of aberrant behaviour?" asked Lord Delaware.

And Sir James confirmed that he believed this to be the case, and that he *naturally* would have no objection to any course of action that his Lordship might suggest. And so the girl was taken to lie down in his room; to reflect, to sob, to start to put her whipping behind her, and to compose herself before that afternoon's long journey back to Delaware Hall.

Sanctuary lost

Her heart fluttered as they left the motorway. Five miles to go.

Five miles until daddy abandoned her.

Five miles until the horror began again.

The heavy wrought iron gates were the same, of course, although covered in a fresh coat of black paint. They always used to be kept closed, she recalled. (To stop the girls from escaping, it occurred to her to wonder?).

They were open now, but the notice on the wall had changed. No longer proclaiming a welcome to Stonehall Ladies' College.

She wondered how many of the other girls had been brought back - as 'treats' by their lovers? Dared to explore the delights of the recently re-opened, press-acclaimed, ever-so-grand Stonehall Manor Hotel. 'Your luxurious, care-free country bolthole', as it described itself proudly in the glossy press ads.

Care-free?

The long parade of oak trees lining the drive were a few feet taller. The desire to open the door of the moving car, to jump out, to plead to be taken back to safety, love, comfort: that remained unchanged.

Tom wasn't to have known, of course, that the demons that she'd taken such pains to chase away would have heard news of her imminent return and grinned their evil grins: "Coming back, my dear? Coming home?"

And he'd have been mortified, had he known. Tom, dear sweet Tom. Strong Tom, dependable Tom, caring Tom. Devoted Tom. So unlike the succession of assorted bastards, turncoats, svelte liars and needy-but-instantly-regrettable-fumbles who'd preceded him.

No. Time to put on a brave face. I was happy at school. Really. I didn't dance a jig of joy when I heard that the College was closing. I don't wake up in the small hours, sometimes, often, fleeing my tormentors, recoiling from their blows. When I press myself against your warm, forgiving body, it's not that I need sanctuary. Honest.

My tormentors. By which she usually meant the older girls. Christine Amberleigh. Isabel Chappell. Susan Balmain. The others. Those girls. But what of the ones whom she herself had tormented, as she'd tried to impress, to be welcomed as one of the in-crowd? Did they still dream terrified dreams, she often agonised, when she gave in and allowed her mind to wander back.

And what of the members of the Common Room?

What of Mr Gillespie?

All of the ghosts, assembling to confront her once more. And Gillespie's at the head of the queue.

The car scrunched over the gravel, bringing her back to reality. "You can't..." she started, before interrupting herself: the glistening Jaguars and BMWs of today's guests *could*, of course, park in one of the hallowed spots that were formerly the domain of the senior members of the common room's battered old vehicles. Daddy used to be made to park by the stable block: it kept the girls and their tearful farewell embraces out of sight, out of mind. Only her embraces were never tearful: Daddy was too oblivious, she was too embarrassed. She kept her sobs for the dormitory and the dark.

It must look impressive, she guessed, if you hadn't seen it before. The imposing Victorian mansion; the glimpse of the formal gardens; the age-old chapel, rebuilt by Wren in the days when the estate had belonged to Lord Chadwick.

Tom smiled happily at her - checking that his girlfriend was glad to be back. She couldn't tell him: she was a confident young woman now - happy, Miss Successful. She'd made the effort. Conquered the shyness, overcome the hurt. No longer the small, lonely child. At least on the surface.

Her took her hand, smiling happily to himself. His good idea. His little adventure. "Paradise regained, eh?" he teased, squeezing her, as he led her once more through that front door.

The hotel reception. The school admin office. Cold, as ever. The little girl, standing there, yellow slip of paper from her housemaster in hand, waiting for the school secretary to reach down the leather book and transcribe the details. The braver adult, smiling weakly as the receptionist welcomed them. Asked if they'd stayed before as they signed the printed form ("Oh yes," boasted Tom of the former victim who leant her head against him). Pointed them towards the stairs.

She stopped, abruptly. The trophy cabinet, silverware still gleaming. Still here? But of course - where else would they have gone? There can't be much of a market for tarnished trophies from a tarnished school.

"Win any of those, my dear?" Tom enquired. She blushed as she pointed one out: the Hailsham Cup, still recognisable - would they let her get it out, she wondered, smiling for the first time. Her name carved out with those of the other Debating champions. The first, and still only, thing she'd ever won. Apart from Tom.

He tugged her on, towards the main staircase. A red carpet now, but the impressive (albeit slightly tasteless) stained glass still cast its colours across the hallway. Again, she hesitated.

"What is it, my love?"

She feigned a smile. "We weren't allowed to use these stairs."

Training runs deep, when breaking rules had such consequences. (He'll be having me walk on the grass next, she reflected, almost allowing herself a smile. Almost.). Tom giggled, his adventure continuing.

Along the first floor corridor. Past the bedrooms carved out from the dorms in which the older girls chose their prey.

Past Dorm 3. Or, should she say now, room 14. But still the same walls which had watched her and Samantha Moran when they'd... explored. Touched, caressed, tasted; nervously, awkwardly, breathlessly. A wooden chair wedged bravely under the door handle as the others sat in prep. And their shared experience wedged between them thereafter: too embarrassed, too shy ever to repeat - or even acknowledge - their escapade.

Their allotted room was at the end of the landing. Bright, white. Quite as trendy as the papers had said. Unrecognisable. Yet unforgettably familiar; snipped from Dorm 5, where Isabel had taunted, Christine had hit. She drew the curtains, wanting to shut out the world - not wanting yet to look out at the playing fields, scene of twice-weekly humiliations almost as crushing as those of the bullies.

And drew the curtains because she wanted him. Needed him. Needed him to make her safe. Needed him to posses her - to punish her for her ungrateful thoughts. She undressed while he was in the bathroom, climbing under the soft down duvet, for once ashamed of her nakedness. Lay face down, buried in the pillows. Waited for him to climb in next to her. To feel her immobile, and climb on top. To take her, urgently: for his pleasure, this, not hers. To pause. Pin her wrists down. Then to possess his schoolgirl, deeply, intimately, in the way she so needed.

"Bet you never did this while you were here before," he grinned afterwards. Not this, not exactly, she thought, remembering Sam Moran once again. Remembering Jason Walker, the groundsman's son, up in Higher Stonehall Woods; she wondered what had become of him. If only you knew, dear Tom, if only you knew.

But, sated, he was asleep. His girl taken, job done.

She slid from the bed, leaving her lover to his snores and his dreams. The bathroom tiles were cold against her feet. She eyed up the deep bath, freestanding in the centre of the floor; they'd share that later, she thought, and then take each other once more. But now she simply wanted to shower, to try to wash away the memories.

Biggest improvement so far, she thought, as the hot water streamed down her, although the row of cold showers and shivering girls, watched over by the too-dutiful staff, might have made an interesting spectacle for today's moneyed guests. How many of them realised what it had been like, she wondered, beneath the new and all too superficial gloss?

She dried herself quickly. Back in the room, Tom was dreaming deeply; she loved the way his limbs flickered in his sleep, cat-like. She steadied herself, closing her eyes, thinking, always thinking; if only she could stop. If only she could climb back in next to her protector; to safety; to love.

But there was somewhere she knew she had to go. She picked up her crumpled clothes, abandoned so hurriedly at Tom's orders, and dressed.

Am I brave enough?

I need to see.

Do I dare?

I have to...

Hands trembling, she opened the bedroom door, and set off along the corridor. The stairs led upwards, towards more gleaming, polished rooms, before they twisted up one more, narrow flight.

She hesitated. And started to climb.

Aged fifteen, now. Palms sweating. Counting the stairs, willing them to continue for ever. Finding herself all too suddenly on the small landing outside her housemaster's attic room.

Composing herself. Knocking on his door, softly. No answer. Knocking again, more forcefully: let me in. Let me flee.

The realisation that Gillespie wasn't there. One-thirty, he'd said. After lunch. Not that she'd eaten. One twenty-nine now.

Minutes ticking by. Long, silent minutes.

The loneliest minutes in a girl's life.

Contemplating. Regretting. Anticipating. Trying to imagine what it would be like; trying not to imagine too hard.

At last, hearing footsteps climbing the stairs. Standing straight, as if a correct posture would save her from harm.

Not him, though. Eleanor Cameron, instead. Lower Sixth; another star pupil. Two unfamiliar lunchtime visitors to these quarters, lining up, barely acknowledging one another, each lost in her own fears.

Heavier steps this time. Drawing near, in slow-motion. As though they were in a movie - although one in which other girls were supposed to star.

Gillespie scrabbled for the key in his coat pocket, and swung open the door. "I'll speak to Miss Cameron first."

Unfair, unfair, as the other girl brushed past. I was here first. Me, sir. Minutes more to fret - yet minutes more unscathed, too.

Through the door, she heard the murmur of voices, which fell into a long, ominous silence. A silence full of expectation, punctuated by a crack and an anguished howl. Her mind circled like a carousel, trying to picture the scene; trying to block it.

Four evenly-spaced whacks in all, each driving out its yelp of anguish and apology, then a silence once more. More murmuring... and then, before she knew it, the door was opening, and the first victim was making her escape, and she was passing - avoiding Eleanor's eyes at all costs - and the door was closing behind her. And she was standing small in front of her housemaster.

"A petty act," she heard. "Destructive. Infantile. Susan was most distressed". Susan was distressed? About her books being left to soak in the shower? Susan, chief tormentor? And how did Susan feel when she was punching, kicking, scratching? But revenge was to have its due price: three strokes of the cane, recognising that she was a generally well-behaved girl who'd stepped momentarily out of line.

Her fingers trembled so much she could hardly manage to remove her knickers, before she bent over as instructed, lifting the grey skirt up and over her back, baring herself to him. "Touching toes without flinching", as he whipped the rod down bringing pain as yet unimaginable, unbearable. The first stroke shocked her; the second astonished her; the third broke her, tears flooding out and shoulders heaving as she somehow maintained her stance.

And then she was on her way, shamed and shocked, punishment slip in hand. All done, all forgotten (although even as he said it, Gillespie must have known that *not* to be the case. Not then. Not ever.)

And now. What, a little more than a decade on?

The hotel guest lent back against the corridor wall, hands against the cool paint. Breathed deeply. Rubbed her watering eyes. She was almost congratulating herself on having brought herself back to confront the demons, when the door opened. Instinctively she stood to attention, but a smartly-dressed woman appeared: the same age, a little older perhaps, but somehow familiar. Looking at her with not a little concern and asking whether she needed help.

She forced a smile. "I'm fine. I got lost. It's a bit of a warren, isn't it. And all those stairs..." They nodded, they paused, and she was left alone once more.

She waited until the other woman was safely away, before heading back. Easier this time than then, when the veil of tears and the pain and the humiliation and her shaking legs had made the staircase harder to descend than a Himalayan peak. This time her backside simply ached from Tom's ministrations, and her mind blazed merely (*merely?*) with her memories.

That time, she'd had to return to the admin office, the yellow punishment slip which Gillespie had completed to be passed to the curious secretaries to be recorded in the Punishment Book for posterity. (And what would have happened to the Punishment Book, she wondered, when the school was forced to close? Burnt, she hoped, with all of its shameful stories of bared backsides and bruised pride. Not in someone's trophy cabinet, she prayed. God forbid, not still in the hotel).

This time, she could head back to the bedroom and strip to crawl in with Tom. That time, she had to lie face down on the hard dormitory bed, skirt raised, hands inside her panties, hardly able to touch the raised, burning skin.

This time, Tom reached a protective arm around her, too sleepy to notice the tears that flow from conquering demons. That time the tears were on all-too-public display. Taunts of "Look what we've got here," echoed around. She remembered hoping that Eleanor, in another dorm along the corridor, was being cuddled and consoled; remembered wishing that they could change places.

At least some of the bullying had stopped; a caned paragon of virtue was at least a real girl. In her no-longer-iconic state, she'd found herself watching from safety as the bullies meted out their hateful treatment, no longer the one on the receiving end. After a few evenings as a spectator, she'd even - to her surprise, her shame, and her astonished enjoyment - joined in, using her wit to tease and taunt, the words scything into the victims even as she pummelled them. One of the gang, now.

After you'd been flogged once, so rumour foretold, future whippings no longer held the same terror. She could vouch that this was untrue: she'd been back in Gillespie's study early the following term, howling her way through another dreadful six strokes. Six strokes for bullying, plus two more for flinching. "Obviously I was overly-generous last time," he'd observed as she'd implored him for mercy. She'd cried like a baby for hours afterwards, less from the caning than from the guilt - her career as a wannabe bully now firmly ended.

But that was then, and this was now. And Tom was there, and was stirring, and was holding her and stroking her. He hadn't even noticed that she'd been away. She'd never told him; never would. Couldn't let down her guard, let the mask slip, reveal the fragile little girl underneath. Successful now. She'd survived. She'd won. Hadn't she?

And after all, everyone enjoys their schooldays.

Don't they?

The girl behind the counter

The girl behind the counter glanced around the coffee shop. Mid-morning: the usual mix. Students, installed on their favourite sofas, eking out their late-breakfast small skinny cappuccinos. Businesspeople too spendthrift or junior to hire an office, convening instead in the quieter corners with their mochas and their smoothies.

And then there were those customers waiting to visit the establishment across the street. The young women toying with their drinks, staring into the distance. Nervous. Scared. Glancing at their watches every tenth second, lest they be late for their appointment at the WJPC.

The Women's Judicial Punishment Centre. Most were alone - too ashamed to tell parents, friends, lovers of their crime and of their sentence. A few gentlemen, a few girlfriends sat amidst the soon-to-be-flogged lasses. Some sympathetic, offering comforting cuddles. A few stern: "How dare you end up *here*?"

Ten to eleven: movement in the ranks. It could take no more than two minutes to cross the road, yet tardiness was unthinkable. Once the first girl had moved to the door, the rest inevitably followed - studiously avoiding each other's eyes. Sharing a fate, yet resolutely remaining strangers.

The few guardians, compatriots, tidied their tables, headed out to pace the streets and wait.

A lull descended; the girl behind the counter busied herself clearing cups ready for the new arrivals.

Five to eleven: the welcoming party for the previous batch appeared on cue.

At two minutes past eleven, sharp: the tearful arrivals from the ten o'clock brigade reappeared. Shame-faced, holding fiery, thrashed backsides. Looking around for cushions, and for comfort if there was anyone to offer it. Looking around at anyone except those who had just shared their agonising fate.

The girl behind the counter glanced at her watch, studied their expressions, as if the details of their experience could be read in their tears. What precisely went on across the street?

Could it be quite as awful as it appeared to be? To be birched: twenty strokes, for a first offence. On the bare. "To punish you and to protect society from future offences." She'd heard that the officers laid it on hard after the offender had been tied into position: that even the bravest amongst the girls broke.

The clock ticked on. Punished girls dried their eyes, slowly regained their composure - or pretended to. Departed to rejoin the world outside, to try to forget - although their stripes would continue to remind them for some time. And the memories would never fade.

Before long, their midday replacements soon started to shuffle in, preparing themselves for their appointments with the coffee shop's neighbours. Drinking, yet not drinking.

The girl behind the counter glanced at her watch again. Looked around nervously at her co-workers. Took a cloth; cleaned the tables she'd polished just a few minutes previously. Polished them again, just to be sure. To pass the time.

High noon? Not long to go, now.

Glanced at her watch. Went into the back room. Washed her face in cold water, slipped off her coffee shop T-shirt and apron, buttoned up her smart blouse. Her best blouse.

Ten to midday. The first of the offenders headed for the door. She watched the others follow, seeing the dread in their faces.

She fumbled in her pocket: the letter was still there. The girl slipped from behind the counter. Joined the back of the procession. She'd be back in a little more than an hour. Just a short trip across the road. She'd try to be one of the brave ones, even if her eyes were already starting to water as she shut the coffee shop door behind her.

The punishment list

Sunday, 11.45am

Alice wanted to turn. Turn and run, down the stairs, out of the door, down the school's long drive and away. To escape. To safety.

But she knew she couldn't: that fleeing would only make things worse. That she'd only be brought back, later, to stand here again – outside the library door, dreading what was to happen. Yet at the same time not knowing exactly what was to happen: that was the worst part.

That the punishment would hurt – that was for sure. That was the easy part to comprehend. How much, she didn't know. Almost, didn't care. It couldn't be that bad – could it? Or could it? Would she be able to cope without making a fool of herself? To retain some dignity in this awful predicament.

But the humiliation – of being ordered here, like a naughty child. With everyone knowing – everyone in the school aware that their proud, intelligent, attractive, confident and usually oh-so-well-behaved head girl was to be disciplined at this very moment.

And the total, abject lack of control. That for the next five, ten minutes (how long would it take? How long before it would be all over, before she'd be free?) – that for the next few minutes, there would be nothing she could do other than to obey whatever instructions she was given; to be meek, mild, to submit.

She steadied herself, noticing her hands shaking as she brushed her dress, making sure she looked tidy. And then, heart fluttering, she knocked gently on the heavy, wooden door.

"Come in..."

Four days earlier: Wednesday, 8.30am

Green was in a bad mood. A very bad mood. It always happened, of course, at this time of year. The start of May. Most of the school year completed, in that strange period before exams started when the need to study contrasted with the delights of wandering outside in the glorious sun.

And yet this year, somehow, the balance was wrong. Too much of that lazing around in the summer sunshine. Too many pupils missing lessons. Too many reports of sixth-formers being seen in local pubs – even of younger students out in the next town, fifteen miles away, in the middle of the school day (although how they had got there, goodness knew).

Well, it was time to lay down the law. He walked towards the assembly hall, scarcely acknowledging his deputy head and the head boy and girl as they fell in behind their headmaster and he strode through the hall, up onto the stage and looked down on the pupils of Ridgewood College.

He watched them as they sang the morning hymn: half-heartedly, discordant. Half of them wearing their blazers, half not. Untidy. Ill-disciplined. Well, he'd had enough.

The popular consensus afterwards was that none of the students had ever seen Green look so annoyed. He lectured them on the importance of their exams, of their need to repay the investment that their parents had made in their education. He bemoaned their appearance: "scruffy clothes are the result of a scruffy mind". He tore into them for damaging the reputation of the school in the local area by their truancy and misconduct.

And he gated them. All of them. "No-one is to leave the school premises without the express prior, written permission of a member of staff. I've had enough of truancy, and intend to stamp it out." Black and white. Clear cut. Not even to buy sweets in the local shop.

And the final warning. "The next few weeks will see this school be a serious place. A place of learning. A place of study. A place of quiet, mature behaviour. And woe betide anyone who steps out of line, for I will punish them with the utmost severity."

Well, the threat was there. Plain, for all to note.

And he would, too. Green was usually a tolerant man – soft, some would say (although never to his face). But it was well known that corporal punishment, although rarely used these days, was there as a last resort – and which of them was going to risk that?

The previous Wednesday, 5pm

She turned up the volume on her car stereo, pulling out to overtake yet another line of dawdling drivers. Glorious sunshine. A great day for hitting the road – especially in her red open-top Beetle. Being allowed a car at school was one of the better privileges of being head girl, Alice thought to herself. And of coming from a well-off background, of course: not many girls were given a convertible for passing their driving test!

The rapidly-approaching van almost caught her off guard, and she just managed to cut back into her lane, horns sounding as other drivers showed their annoyance at her. She gestured, rudely, at the car behind – didn't he realise that driving fast was part of the fun of a sports car?

Soon, Alice reached the edge of the high, stone wall that marked the boundary of the school. Back to reality, back to boredom – back to studying for her A Levels in three weeks' time. She braked sharply, flinging the car to the right through the school gates, the gravel scrunching underneath the wheels as she tore down the drive. She threw the vehicle into a vacant parking space, pressed the button to close the electronic roof, and threw her cap and sunglasses onto the seat.

She glanced at her watch – just after five. Damn, she thought – she had to supervise an hour's homework for the first year students. Just what she didn't want…

Wednesday – a little later

"Did Green find you?"

Alice turned around. Matthew caught up with her: "He was looking for you about ten minutes ago. I told him I thought you were in the library." She looked at her – well, not quite boyfriend… her best friend, smiling at him.

"I was. I had to supervise it for an hour. Did he say what it was about?"

"Nope. Still looks in a foul mood, though."

"Wonder what's got into him?"

"Sunstroke?" They both laughed. Matt did that – made her laugh. He was fun – a good companion, someone with whom she could sort out the world's problems, and a useful if very occasional shoulder to cry on. And nothing more. Despite what any of the rumours might say. A strictly platonic relationship. At the moment.

"Well," she said, "I'd better go and hunt down the terrible ogre – see what he's after. See you."

"Bye. See you at dinner?"

"Yep. Unless his lordship sends me off on some errand!"

"As if…"

"As if! Must go." She danced off, happy. She wondered where the headmaster would be. Dinner was twenty minutes away, so he'd be somewhere around. If Matt had told Green that she was in the library, he may well have gone that way. And then when she hadn't been there, he'd probably have gone on to his study.

She skipped up the stairs, turned left and into the school secretary's room. Miss Carter was still there, and looked up.

"Evening, Miss Carter. Is Dr. Green in?"

She looked up, solemn. "He is, Alice. Although he's not in a very good mood, I should warn you. But go on in." She pressed the buzzer: "Alice Meadows to see you, headmaster."

Alice rapped on the door and entered. Green was standing by the window, silhouetted against the sunlight. He turned round. Sternly: "I've been looking for you."

"I know, sir. Matthew told me. I thought I might find you here."

"Sit down." He pointed to the armchair. Wow, she thought to herself, as he walked round and sat opposite her on the leather sofa, he WAS in a bad mood!

Green continued: "Do you know why I wanted to see you, Alice?"

"Erm... no. But let me know and I'll be happy to oblige."

"Stop being frivolous. I'm not in the mood. Well, if you're not prepared to hazard a guess, let me ask you this: since when has the head girl been above the law in this school?"

"Pardon?" Alice thought fast. What was he talking about?

"I asked you to let me know when it was that we decided that our head girl could disobey school rules?"

"I don't know what you mean, sir."

"You were in assembly this morning?"

"Yes, sir." She tried to rack her brains. Assembly? What had she done wrong in assembly? "What did I do wrong?"

"Well, I'd hope that what you did wrong was not to listen. Otherwise I'll be even more annoyed."

"I.... I don't understand." There must be some confusion.

"Listen, girl, I've just had a meeting with a gentleman who was considering sending his son and daughter to the school next year. And he wasn't very happy. Said that he was reconsidering his decision. Said that he had been concerned about the standards of behaviour here."

She looked puzzled. "And what has this got to do with me not listening in assembly, Dr. Green? I'm sorry, but I don't understand."

"Apparently, when he was about half a mile from the school this afternoon, he was overtaken by a young girl in a red sports car. Who was driving dangerously, and who – to use his words –

'gave him the finger' when he let her in to avoid a van that was coming the other way as she overtook."

"Oh...."

"And he then turned into the school and parked, and saw said red sports car in the car park and a young lady very much fitting your description getting out of it."

"Oh...."

He leant forward, looking at her in the eyes. "So what do you have to say other than 'oh', Alice?"

"I... I ... Well, he must have been mistaken. I did go out for a drive, and I do remember waving to thank someone for letting me in when I was overtaking, just before I got back to the school gates, but I wouldn't have made a rude gesture. Honestly, I wouldn't."

Green paused. "You went out for a drive?"

"Yes.... I felt like some fresh air. I didn't go far."

"So you weren't listening this morning? Or did you have permission?"

"I'm sorry?"

"Well if you had been listening, you would have heard me saying that no pupil was allowed off the school premises without written permission."

Momentary panic. "I was listening. And I did hear. But. I mean. That was for the pupils as a whole. I didn't think it covered me."

"Why? Are you somehow above the law?"

This was awful. "No, sir. But, I guess, there's all sorts of things I do as head girl that are different to everyone else."

"Absolutely. And which of those are in direct contradiction of school rules, and which go flatly against an unequivocal policy I announced only a few hours before in assembly?"

She paused, and stared at the carpet. "None. Look, I'm sorry, sir. It won't happen again. I promise. I guess I just didn't think."

"Well, I'm glad it won't happen again. And thank you for the apology." Green stood up, and walked to his desk, taking out his fountain pen and scribbling something on a piece of paper. He folded it, put it into an envelope and sealed it.

As Alice stood up, Green walked back over to her. "However, on this occasion, an apology is not enough. When I spoke in assembly this morning, I made it very clear that anyone who disobeyed me would be punished severely." He handed her the envelope. "Please give this to Miss Carter on your way out, or leave it on her desk if she's gone." And he turned and walked away.

Alice was in a daze. She felt her bottom lip tremble, her cheeks flushing. This was unreal. "But sir. I mean, I'm the head girl. It was a mistake. I've apologised... Please." She looked across at the headmaster, desperate, blinking back tears.

"I am not going to let a pupil – *any* pupil, even if she is the head girl – undermine me within a day of me making myself clear in assembly. You'd better look at the main noticeboard on Friday when we publish the Punishment List for the week. You can expect me to have taken the fact that you are head girl into full account when determining the punishment that I have chosen to award. Now leave."

"Sir..." She looked at him again, but he had sat down at his desk and started to write. Shell-shocked, she turned away. The Friday notice went up every week listing the worst offenders – and their punishments: usually a weekend detention, but occasionally worse. The notice usually left three sections blank – expulsions, suspensions and... and corporal punishment.

"Punish severely"... Surely not...?

She was shaking as she went out of the door. The secretary had left, so Alice placed the envelope on her desk, desperate to open it and see what Green had written. But that would make it worse. Much worse. So she walked away, composing herself, out into the corridor, and fled as quickly as she could to her bedroom, where she lay on the bed and burst into tears.

Alice walked around the school as if in a daze for the next two days, terrified of her potential fate. Matt had been reassuring when he came and found her in her room on the Wednesday evening: Green would be fine about it. That the head knew she'd done a good job as head girl; that he was just trying to scare her. That he would realise that even by giving her a weekend detention, and publicising it on the school noticeboard, he'd be humiliating her enough.

And yet. And yet. She knew deep down that that was not the only option. That infrequent as the use of corporal punishment was on girls in the school – once every three, four years perhaps – Green had been very angry. And that even if he'd calmed down, he'd written that note for his secretary at the height of his anger. Alice tried to recall how much she'd seen Green write, trying to guess what he might have written, picturing the envelope that she'd placed on Miss Carter's desk, the envelope in which her fate was sealed.

And what if it was worse still - if he expelled her? Suspended her, at this critical time before her A Level exams? All she'd worked for at school could be under threat, her promised place at Cambridge included. And her stepfather... no, Alice shuddered to think how he might re-act if she was sent home. She remembered that time aged 15, when he'd found a pack of cigarettes in her room; pictured him unbuckling his belt and sliding it out, bending it in two. And only her mother's pleadings had saved her. Yet this time... no, it wasn't worth thinking about.

Matt was being great. Supportive. Kind. Protective. Yet at the end of the day, there wasn't that much he could do to calm the butterflies in her tummy. Her mind wandered in lessons, drifting over so many regrets: why she hadn't realised Green's edict applied to her; why she had decided to go for that fateful drive. She thought about Matt – kind, sweet Matt, Matt about whom she cared so much and whom she'd miss so much when she went to University. If she ever got to University. Matt who wanted their relationship to be more than 'just friends', but from whom she'd stayed ever so slightly withdrawn, separate, as if scared to take that leap of faith and give in to her emotions.

And she thought about what might happen. How many times did she visualise walking up to that noticeboard on Friday afternoon, checking... yet all she could see in her mind's eye was a blank sheet of paper pinned to the board.

She hardly slept at all. On Wednesday, she finally cried herself to sleep in the early hours of the morning. On Thursday, she tossed and turned for hours, nodding off in her chair at 3 am, History textbook in hand.

And then it was Friday... Punishment List day.

Friday, 3.32pm

She'd looked at the noticeboard several times, of course. The list was always displayed at some point in the afternoon, but the exact time varied from week to week. Alice first looked at 11am, then again after every lesson: trying to be discreet, hoping that noone would sense the cause of her curiosity, of her anxiety.

Double History after lunch was not the easiest of lessons through which to concentrate. The Napoleonic Wars somehow paled into insignificance compared to her own private torment. And as the lesson drew to a close, with it came the ever increasing realisation that the notice might be there at afternoon break.

Her hands were shaking as she picked up her textbook at the end of the class and made her way into the corridor. And then she noticed – Miss Carter climbing the stairs, up towards her office – away from the noticeboards. That could only mean...

Heart fluttering, she galloped downstairs, and spied a group of the younger pupils already standing by the board. As she came into sight, she sensed them stop, look up at her in excitement, then make way as she walked towards the Board to read of her fate:

HEADMASTER'S NOTICE
RIDGEWOOD COLLEGE
PUNISHMENT LIST

WEEK ENDING FRIDAY, 8 MAY

    WEEKEND DETENTIONS
    P. Hyde (Form 3B)
    S. Jones (Form 4A)
    F. Owen (Form 3C)

SUSPENSIONS
None

EXPULSIONS
None

CORPORAL PUNISHMENT
A. Meadows (Upper 6 Arts)

ALL PUPILS APPEARING ON THIS LIST SHOULD CONSULT THE ADJACENT NOTICE FOR FURTHER DETAILS

P.Green
Headmaster

She bit her lip, tears welling up, reading again. 'A. Meadows (Upper 6 Arts)'. *Alice* Meadows. Her. She scanned the more detailed notice. This wasn't happening to her, surely? She read on:

CORPORAL PUNISHMENT

Pupils whose name appear on the list of those to receive Corporal Punishment should report to the School Library immediately following Sunday morning Chapel two days after the publication of the relevant Punishment List. They should wear their usual school uniform.

And then she heard their excited voices. "Is that you, Alice?" "Is there a mistake?" "What did you do?" "Alice is for the whack." "Greenie's going to cane the head girl." "Bend over, Alice." "Come and look everyone…"

She turned and fled, tears dripping down her face, the shame and humiliation too much to bear. She sensed others looking at her as she rushed through the school, wondering what was amiss – knowing that they too would soon learn of her fate. The girls' washroom was just in front of her, and she hurried in, going into a cubicle and shutting the door. She sat down and buried her head in her hands, trying to prevent the sobs from being heard by her neighbours.

And then – and only then – did the shame and humiliation give way to a rising terror of what was really in store for her: of the fact that she was going to be caned. Caned. Thrashed. Flogged. Hurt. But as she started to panic, the bell went, summoning the students back to the final two lessons of the afternoon. She left the cubicle, went to the sink and washed her face in the cold water, trying to make herself look presentable.

"Be brave, Alice," she repeated to herself, as she dried her face and walked into the corridor. Hearing, as soon as she did, the first of the cries that were to haunt her for the next few days: "There she is! What did you do, Alice? Why are you up for the stick? It's going to hurt, you know." She tried to block their jeers out, to stand tall, not to cry. "Be brave, Alice." And she walked into the German classroom, past the staring eyes of her fellow sixth-formers, and sat at her desk as the teacher started the lesson.

Sunday morning, 11.05am

The past day and a half had been terrible. Any vain hope she might have had that her fellow pupils might not notice that she was to be punished, or might be in any way sympathetic, had vanished within the first moments in front of that hateful notice. And aside from Matt and a couple of other good friends, the laughter and teasing had left her bewildered, dismayed. And scared.

And now this. Sat in Chapel, in the prefects' usual row – at the front of the choir stalls, where everyone could see them. And five hundred pairs of eyes, focused solely on her, watching, knowing all about her impending appointment with the headmaster - who was right now standing a matter of feet from her, reading the lesson. Hearing sniggers, as they realised his pointed choice of biblical text, any thought that Green might have forgiven her forgotten as soon as she heard the most oft-quoted line from the passage in question – "Spare the rod and spoil the child."

Matt had tried to reassure her, of course. Had sat up with her through much of the night, talking, trying (without much success) to persuade her to play cards with him, to keep her mind off things. But this morning... she'd just wanted to be on her own. To think. To shower. To put her uniform on, making sure it was carefully pressed, the school blazer on top of the knee-length blue dress that she was entitled, and supposed, to wear to denote her position as head girl. (Unlike the other girls, she noted, whose *black* dresses would allow them to blend into the crowd, even her uniform set her aside, made her visible). Her bare feet in the freshly-polished black sandals that the summer term required.

The service dragged on – but to Alice's mind, that was a good thing - every hymn, every prayer a delay for what was to follow. But soon the chaplain and the headmaster were gathering up their books and processing out of the chapel to the sounds of the organ. As always, the pupils filed out from the back of the church first, leaving the prefects and choir until last. And then, head down, Alice left the building, through the crowds, through the taunts, and walked across the school grounds to the main building and up the stairs towards the Library.

She steadied herself, noticing her hands shaking as she brushed her dress, making sure she looked tidy. And then, heart fluttering, she knocked gently on the door.

'Come in!"

She walked in, trying to appear confident, desperate not to give away her true feelings. The headmaster was seated across the room, behind the librarian's desk, and she noted that the tables in front of it had been moved towards the side, out of the way. And on the desk... her eyes were drawn to the long, wooden stick with its curved handle, to which she was shortly to be so painfully introduced.

There was no chair in front of the desk, so she stood, nervously, her legs shaking.

"I'm not going to waste time lecturing you, Miss Meadows. We both know why you're here. I am furious at your conduct. As you will have seen from the punishment list, I intend to administer corporal punishment to you, to teach you a lesson. Have you anything to say?"

She stumbled over the words, excuses pouring out; clichéd, like the pleas of any naughty girl in her position. "Sir, I'm sorry, sir. I didn't do it deliberately, honestly I didn't."

"Well, I am going to teach you to be a little more deliberate in your compliance with school rules, and I am certainly going to make you sorry. I want you to remove your knickers, place them in your blazer pocket, and then take off your blazer and fold it neatly on the table to your side."

Take off her knickers? But…. surely not?

"Are you waiting for something?"

"No, sir." Stunned, she reached under her dress, and felt for the elastic, pulling the white knickers down and stepping out of them. Fumbling, she stuffed them into her pocket and took off the jacket, laying it down as instructed. He was going to cane her on the bare!

Green opened a large, old, leather-bound book on the table, and took out his fountain pen. He turned to a fresh page, and started to write. "This book retains the details of many decades of pupils who have seriously transgressed, Miss Meadows, but as far as I am aware, none of whom have shared your esteemed position as a head prefect. So this is doubly disappointing for me." He looked up at her, and then down at the leather tome.

"Now then. Name: Alice Meadows. Class: Upper 6 Arts?"

"Yes, sir."

"Date: 10 May. Offence: truancy and wilful disobedience. Implement: senior cane. Strokes: six."

Alice gasped. Six! Green continued. "And for the further offence of rudeness to College guests – that's your gesture to the gentleman you overtook – an additional two strokes. Making eight in all. Now I have very simple rules for this: you bend over and touch your toes. I cane you. You count the stroke and thank me, then stay in position for the next stroke.

Anything different, and the stroke doesn't count: I repeat it and add another one to the overall total as well. Understood?"

Dazed, she nodded.

"Good. Then bare your buttocks and assume the position." Green stood, and picked up the rod.

This was too terrible. Surely he wouldn't cane her on the bare? "What are you waiting for, girl?"

Scarcely able to comprehend what was happening, Alice lifted the back of her skirt and bent forwards, reaching down towards the ground. The headmaster walked behind her, cutting the stick through the air, and moved closer. She felt him tug at the dress, pulling it right up over her back, her buttocks bare, her backside (and she dreaded to think what else) completely exposed.

She flinched as he stepped to the side and measured the cold wooden stick across her. And then.... AND THEN! The swish as the cane cut through the air; the blow almost knocking her forwards. And then the pain. She gasped in shock. Oh the pain. Intense. Burning. A hundred times worse than anything she had expected. She took deep breaths, trying to control herself. And then she remembered: "One, sir, thank you, sir."

He measured the rod out again, lower, pressing into her flesh, before flogging it against her just as hard as the first, the retort of wood against skin filling the air. "Owww... two sir, thank you, sir," she yelped, staring down, focusing intently on the carpet, struggling to prevent herself from standing.

And then the third. Oh my goodness. If she'd never experienced pain like the first two lashes, then this took the girl to new levels of anguish, as the perfect blow striped her buttocks. She drew breath, composing herself, before counting the stroke. "Thank you... sir... three, sir."

The fourth and fifth were just as hard, Alice clenching her fists after each stroke, gasping, trying so hard not to move. She was starting to blink back tears now. "Be brave, Alice," she told herself. "Be brave."

And then she felt the headmaster move slightly, lifting the cane higher, and as the sixth stroke landed there was nothing she could do. Alice leapt up, her hands instinctively reaching behind her. Green rapped her knuckles with the stick, annoyed. "Get over."

"Y..y..yes, sir, sorry, sir. Six, sir. Thank you."

"Not six, girl, it doesn't count. Still five. And the total is up one to nine." WHACK! Almost bowling her over with its force, and finally causing her tears to start to fall. "Six, sir, thank you sir," she yelped, only just getting the words out before the seventh descended. CRACK! Low down, hard, stinging as it hit: unbearable. "S...s...seven thank you, sir. Thank you," the words tumbled out.

Green stepped back. "And of course, that would be it for now if you'd not flinched, girl. But we still have two more to go."

WHIP!

"Aaaaargh. Oh God, no, please, sir. I mean, eight sir, thank you." Alice wriggled her legs, as if trying to shake the pain away, and then concentrated: the last stroke, and then it would all be over. Waiting... sensing Green watching her... lifting the rattan... and delivering the final blow with all of his strength. Yet she hung on, terrified lest she moved, unable to bear the thought of another two blows. And then she counted this final stroke: "Nine, sir, thank you, sir."

Green was already walking back round the table, placing the rod down on the desk and sitting down. "Stand, girl." She reached back and pushed her skirt down, standing up and letting it fall back to her knees, looking at the head through a mist of tears. Her hands strayed behind her, as if the burning pain could be rubbed away. The caning had been awful – far worse than she had imagined, but at least it was now over. All she wanted was to leave, to get back to her room, to be alone.

"That completes your caning for your truancy, disobedience and rudeness, Miss Meadows. Do you understand?"

She nodded. "Yes, sir."

The headmaster continued. "Now then, young lady, place your hands by your side. I want to make one other matter very plain. You're the head girl of this school, and as such I have the right to expect certain standards of behaviour from you. You have fallen far short of those. When I spoke to you on Wednesday, I told you that I would be taking your position into account when I decided what discipline to mete out to you, and

I still intend to do that. So having completed your caning for the initial offences, I now intend to punish you for your betrayal of the trust I placed in you as head girl."

"Sir...?" Surely not. Surely he couldn't? This was too awful...

"I notice that you have on the head girl's blue dress, Miss Meadows. In betraying my trust, you have to my mind forfeited your right to wear that garment, and so for the remainder of your punishment I would ask you to take it off."

Dazed. "Sir?" Remainder of her punishment? Taking the dress off? But...

"Take the damn dress off, Miss Meadows, before you end up in even more trouble. And get rid of your shoes whilst you're about it."

Slowly, fingers trembling, she undid the zip, and took off the garment, letting it fall to the floor, bending double as she reached down to take off her sandals. She gathered them up, and took them to the table next to her blazer, before turning to face him again – one arm wrapping around herself to cover her bare breasts, the other hand reaching down to cover her lower modesty.

"No brassiere on today, Miss Meadows?" the headmaster asked.

She gave a muffled sob. "No, sir. I mean, I don't always." And why hadn't she today, she thought, cursing herself. But never in the countless times she'd turned over the scene of what might happen in her mind these past few days had she imagined being made to strip.

"Well I shall avoid the temptation to check the rule book to see if it's mandatory. Now stop this contortion act. Put your hands on your head if you can't stand straight."

Slowly, she uncovered herself, resting her right hand on top of her left, on top of her head, totally bare now to his gaze.

"Had you been an ordinary pupil, Miss Meadows, the caning I administered would have sufficed. On this occasion, I intend to repeat the punishment to illustrate my displeasure with you. You have enjoyed a range of privileges as head girl, and so it is only right that you should be treated more severely if you have misbehaved."

He looked down at the punishment book, and picked up his pen. Alice watched him, dumbstruck. Green looked up. "I was quite forgetting myself, young lady. We need to finish the paperwork for your first caning before we can start this one. So, we have one remaining offence in there: 'Flinching, senior cane, two additional strokes.' Come here and sign to acknowledge receipt of your punishment." He turned the volume around and handed her the pen, which she took, shaking like a leaf. She scribbled as close an approximation as she could to her signature, before stepping back, hands again on her head.

"Now. Let's add this second punishment as a separate entry. Name, Alice Meadows. Class – Upper 6 Arts. Date: 10 May. Offence: Failing to meet behaviour standards expected of the head girl. Implement: senior cane. Same number of strokes as before – let me see now: six, seven-eight, nine... ten."

Alice swayed on her feet. "Please, sir," she pleaded. "You can't. I'm really sorry." Her worst nightmares weren't just coming true – they had been left long behind, and she had no idea how she was going to get through the next few minutes.

"I can and I'm going to." Green stood up, walked round the desk and pulled over a high-backed wooden chair from under one of the tables. "I will, however, be generous and let you get over this for your second thrashing. Otherwise exactly the same rules apply. So stand here, bend right over, and place your hands on the seat of the chair."

Taking her hands off her head, Alice moved into position, her nudity now forgotten in the face of the further humiliation that was to be inflicted on her. She leant forward, her hips touching the top of the wooden back of the chair, and waited.

Again, the dreaded stick tapped her behind, as her tormentor took careful aim. CRACK! The blow landed, straight across the centre of her buttocks, re-igniting the early fires. She bit her lip: "One, sir, thank you, sir."

He paused, waiting, as she stared ahead. A long pause – almost as if he was going to take his time, to enjoy her discomfort. And then he whipped her again. "Aah! No... Two, sir, thank you, sir."

Again the pause. The rod lined up. Four gentle taps. And then back, and then down, and then the by-now-familiar anguish. Through clenched teeth: "Three, sir, thank you, sir."

If anything, the next was the hardest stroke of any to date, and she cried aloud in agony, before subsiding into sobs. "Four, please, sir, no more, thank you, sir, please…"

WHACK! (Don't flinch, don't flinch, stay in position). "Oh God, oh no, please… six, sir thank you sir."

"You miscounted, girl. You're still on five."

"Sorry, sir, I didn't mean…. Owwwwwwwwwwww…." (Be brave, Alice, be brave). "That's six now sir, thank you sir, please sir…."

And then a low one. Hard. Loud. Agonising. (Stay down, don't move, don't let him beat you.) S…sss…ss… seven, sir, thank you, sir." She glanced backwards, with horror, as the headmaster walked several paces back, swishing the cane through the air, then raised it high and started to canter forward. (Be brave, stay still, don't flinch). "Aaaaaaaarrrgh. No, please, no more, sir, sorry, thank you, sir, eight sir, oh no….."

Green stood behind her, watching, as if weighing up his options. "Two to go, girl." And then he delivered the blow that she couldn't take, couldn't bear, that brought her howling to her feet, hands clenching her buttocks, sobbing openly and loudly.

He spoke clearly: "But that one doesn't count, and you now have an extra stroke too, young lady. Three to go." And as she took her position again, he delivered another almighty CRACK!

And again she rose to her feet, shoulders heaving with sobs: "Please, sir, I've had enough. No more. Please."

"Well with the extra stroke again, I think we have four more to go, actually." She listened in horror, knowing that not only had she received her second ten blows, but that the agony was to continue.

Green moved round her, and pulled away the chair, gesturing to the large, oak desk. "So we're not here all day, can I suggest that you bend over that and clutch the far side – and don't let go?" Alice moved forward, leaning over, rising onto tiptoes and reaching forward at full stretch.

"I shall make these quick. No counting. No flinching. Understood?"

"Sir, yes, I do. Understand. Yes, sir."

WHACK! High up, right on one of the most painful of the earlier bruises. TWHACK! (Oh goodness, please, no, stay down, be brave, Alice, be...) CRACK! (...brave, oh no, please, that was as bad as any of them, don't flinch, whatever you do don't flinch, Alice, be brave) and...

So hard....burning... "Aaaaaaaaaaaaaaaaaaaaaargh." (deep breath, sob, deep breath) "Thank you, sir, sorry, sir. Thank you."

"Stand up! Hands on your head again." The headmaster walked round the table as she tried to compose herself, to stop crying, to pull herself together. He drew the leather punishment book towards him, and added in another line: "Flinching. Four additional strokes" before handing her the pen to sign. Shakily, unsteadily, she wrote her name. Wiping the tears away. Realising that for ever more, people would see the details of her ordeal in black and white. The first ten. Then the second, awful caning – fourteen, it must have been. Twenty-four in all. And she'd worried about six.

He was addressing her again. "I hardly need to say that this is not a meeting that I would care to have to repeat, young lady."

He leant forward. "I also have to say that I am very disappointed in you for not taking your punishment more bravely – flinching so many times really is very poor. I'd have thought you'd have more control, more self-esteem."

She sobbed again, his words biting just as much as the cane. "I'm sorry, sir. I meant to be brave."

"Mmmm. Well, even in the way you took your caning, Miss Meadows, you have let yourself down. But as you have taken your punishment, I am going to allow you to continue as head girl – so you'd better get dressed and go."

"Yes, sir, thank you sir." She stepped to the table, pulling on her dress first, shoes next, then her blazer. She wiped her eyes with her arm, trying in vain to make herself look presentable. And then she turned to face the headmaster: "Thank you, sir. Thank you for caning me. And I'm sorry I was bad."

He pointed to the door. "Leave. Now. And don't ever let me see you in here again in these circumstances."

She walked out of the door, into the empty corridor, hands reaching behind her. But no, she thought, I can't stop and cry here.

She walked quickly away, taking the back stairs, hoping not to be seen by anyone. But as she climbed the stairs at the other end, up towards her room, two of the fifth-form boys blocked her way: "Oh look, it's little Miss Cane. How was it for you, darling?" they mocked, as she pushed past them, onwards, up to her floor of the building, and along the corridor to her room.

And then she threw herself onto her bed, and gave in to deep sobs, her hands gingerly reaching down to her hot, swollen buttocks, whilst her mind raced. Humiliated. All pride vanished. And a school full of pupils, who knew exactly what had been done to her behind that closed library door, to face when she could pluck up the courage.

Be brave, Alice. Be brave...

The occupation

Their orders had been clear: catch the girls seen running away from the burning storeroom and make an example of them.

They'd met with the usual wall of silence to start with, naturally. Four months into the occupation, the villagers still refused to co-operate with the soldiers who'd taken their land – and who would willingly hand over two of their girls to these brutes?

Their commander had come up with the solution: the young women of the village had been rounded up, gathered into the market square.

"The miscreants will identify themselves – NOW!"

Silence.

He glared at them: still silence.

"We can do this the easy way, or I can make you comply," he barked.

Still silence.

The officer surveyed the crowd, then grasped one of its number roughly by the hands and pulled her into the open. "Strip her and tie her to the post," he commanded the men at his side. They complied, enthusiastically. She was a pretty thing – the daughter of the village innkeeper, he realised. She'd do.

"Bring me my riding crop".

The girl was pleading, now. "It wasn't me, sir."

"Of that I have little doubt. So tell me who it was."

"No, sir."

"You can't, or you won't?"

She remained silent. "Then I shall see if I can loosen your tongue. And I rather doubt that the guilty parties will stand there and let me whip first you for their crimes, then each of the others in the crowd."

And he brought the implement down, smartly, across her buttocks. She screamed. A second stroke followed, then more, in rapid succession, before a commotion behind him made him stop. Two girls had stepped forward: "Leave her alone. We did it."

The officer walked up close to the tied girl, and spoke into her ear. "Consider yourself lucky, young lady. You disobeyed my order: if you ever do that again, you'll learn the feeling of a proper whipping." He shouted to his men: "Untie this one. Take the other two to the punishment wing in the castle, and flog them until you are sure that their future conduct will be impeccable."

--

She would have been scared witless, in the old days, had she been brought to the castle under arrest to be flogged. A common criminal, humiliated, under the most severe of sentences.

But the war had changed that: torching the occupiers' storerooms had been a duty, an honourable act. There was no shame in this, only pride and defiance.

Even if pride and defiance couldn't quite save her from trembling, from her eyes widening as she looked at the birch in the soldier's hand... They'd tied her tightly over the wooden frame; the ropes bit into her wrists, her ankles. She glanced at her friend, also naked, handcuffed to one of the men in the corner of the room – being made to watch, knowing her turn would come.

Nor did pride and defiance stop the shock, or the sting, as the rod cut against her. They paused, as if expecting that the stroke would draw a response: she wouldn't give them the pleasure.

The next few she bore with surprising ease. By the sixth, she was biting her lip. By the time she lost count, she was scarcely able to contain her cries as the pain grew unbearable. And still they continued, a second soldier taking over lest the first had grown tired.

"Long live the revolution!" She could remain silent no more, and the oath was the best thing she could think to utter without giving in and showing defeat. And, of course, she knew that these ill-educated soldiers spoke not a word of her language, and would be utterly ignorant of the insults that answered their every blow.

"Death to the occupiers!"

"Freedom will be ours!"

"Your king is a whore!"

The soldier with the birch paused, and strode over to her friend in the corner of the room. "What is she saying?"

"She's apologising, sir. Begging you to stop."

"Good." He returned to his place behind her, and lifted the birch once more. "Then she can beg for a little longer."

"We will oust the occupiers!"

"Liberation will come soon!"

"Fight for justice!"

And then the thrashing stopped, and she felt herself being unbound, and lifted up, and taken to the corner of the room by a soldier. His hands wandered over her naked body far more than was necessary, but the excruciating pain of the birching was such that she scarcely noticed.

Time for the second girl to be whipped. A fresh birch; the same ceremony. She bucked and writhed against the binds of the bench rather more than her friend had done. Yet she too remained defiant – silent, not letting them win, then (when the pain became too all-encompassing for silence) crying out their messages of insubordination.

"We will never be defeated!"

"Your cities will burn in our revenge!"

"Your soldiers are cowards!"

"STOP!" A man's voice this time, not hers, as the commander – who'd entered the room quietly, unnoticed, stepped forward. "HOW DARE YOU?!"

For, unlike his men, the officer explained, *he* was completely bilingual. He spoke menacingly. "Perhaps you should have checked whether we would understand, before insulting us like this?"

"I don't care... I would say it anyway."

He carefully removed his cap and jacket, passing them to one of his men. He slowly, neatly rolled up the right sleeve of his crisp white shirt. "Give me the rod!"

It only took three of his strokes before she was sobbing for mercy; six before he requested a fresh birch; twelve before that too lay in shreds across the floor and he ordered his men to release her from the bench.

"Did the first girl behave in a similar way?"

"Yes, sir."

"I see. Then take them both to the cells."

--

An empty, windowless room, behind a bolted iron door.

Cold stone, damp to the touch.

Dark. Pitch dark, save for the flickering of a torch at the far end of a corridor.

The weals from their flogging: angry, tormenting, the pain barely subsiding.

Water, brought in hours after they'd reached the point of craving a drink. Handed over to the girls in silence, the solider laughing as some spilled.

The occasional stale piece of bread thrown in for them to eat. The hunger – tolerable at first – soon almost overwhelming.

And each other, to hold tight, as they relived the anguishes just past – and dreaded what might come next.

Time passing. But how long? Hours, surely? Days turning to nights outside, back to days, unnoticed in this dank dungeon.

Sleep, on the hard floor. Or nightmares, to be precise. Waking in each other's arms, always in tears.

And then the guard was at the door, shining a light in their faces and ordering them to their feet.

The commander wanted to see them, it seemed. For that they needed to be washed: the cold water from the hose cleansed but shocked. Clothes? No. They wouldn't be needed, he explained.

Men suddenly surrounded them – in front, behind, urging them up flights of stairs. They stumbled: "Quickly! Don't keep him waiting."

When they emerged into the light, the contrast between the stone cells and the opulence of the castle's grand rooms was stunning. Grand paintings filled the walls; tapestries, furniture hewn from ancient oaks filled the eyes as they were marched along the corridor. Soft rugs gave comfort to their aching feet. And then they were ushered through a door, which closed firmly behind them, and found themselves face to face before the man responsible for their torments – and their fate.

Not just the commander, however. For at the distant end of the room, tied over a table, was a girl. She faced away from them, nude, whimpering. The cane strokes striping her buttocks were clearly freshly-administered.

He let them take in the scene, then spoke – calmly, his tone not unkind. "You see around you the opulence in which your former rulers lived, whilst your families toiled to make them rich. This is why we liberated your people, and this is why your conduct last week could not go unpunished."

That they had exchanged one oppressor for another crossed both girls' minds, but neither dared speak.

"And so you were flogged, and imprisoned, and I believe that to be fair and just punishment for your arson attack." He walked around them, inspecting their backsides, the marks of the birchings still fresh.

"But then we come to your conduct whilst you were being dealt with by my men. And how to deal with it. I will not have girls utter insults like that in my castle, or anywhere in the area that I now govern. Do I make myself clear?"

They stared at the floor.

"I can't hear you."

"Yes." Faintly, from each, as if the very word would make them choke.

"Yes, SIR!" he bellowed.

"Yes, sir." Spitting out their compliance.

"And so I reflected on how to punish you for your outpourings of invective. Should I have you birched again, I wondered? On the face of it, the most logical option. Yet you have experienced that already. Would a second thrashing within a few days do any more to discipline you? I rather doubt it..."

"But a lesson still needed to be taught, and one of which the villagers would take heed." The officer walked to the far end of the room, picking up a cane and positioning himself behind the tied girl. "I believe Maria here is your best friend."

"*Maria*?!" they sobbed simultaneously. It couldn't be... He wouldn't...?

He measured the stick carefully. "Collective responsibility. One of the villagers insults us: all of the villagers have insulted us. And watching Maria be caned will doubtless be far more instructive for you than flogging each of you again. She's had her first dozen already, and took them rather bravely. Now it's time for her second twelve."

The two girls ran forward, as if to stop him, but the doors burst open the moment the officer called for the, "Guards!"

Order restored. "Hold them tight. And make sure they watch."

And then the caning began. Rattan lifted high. Four smart steps forward. Stroke whipped down. Walking away as their friend screamed, then fought the pain. Turning, running forward to stripe her again.

By the time it was almost done, he asked the tied girl how many strokes were left. He knew the answer, of course. But her mumbled guesses – "Two, three, sir?" – left him unimpressed. "If you don't know, then we'd better rely on my counting, hadn't we. Six more." Making 26 in total, but by now individual cane lines had long started blurring into each other.

He let them dress, afterwards, the guards having brought fresh dresses into the room for each of the three girls. And only then did he allow Maria to join her friends; only then did he choose to glance away as they hugged; only then did he order the guards to take them to the castle gates and release them. Back to the village.

Back to the Resistance. Back to planning his overthrow.

The green slip

Her hands trembled as she handed over the green slip of paper. Miss Jobson peered up at her, trying to conceal her surprise: Miranda Watson wouldn't exactly have topped the headmaster's secretary's list of the girls most likely to have to present herself in these particular circumstances.

"Do you have a Caning Record already, Miranda?" the administrator enquired doubtfully in her faint Yorkshire accent, as she pushed back her chair ready to sort though the filing cabinets. Had she been more composed, the girl might have remarked on the touch of sympathy in Miss Jobson's voice. As it was, the question seemed more like another push on her fall from grace.

Of course not. There'd be papers about her in the neatly-catalogued files, no doubt. Proud accounts of her contribution to famous sporting victories over rival girls' public schools. Photos at the curtain call of some resounding success of a school play. Copies of glowing end-of-term reports.

But no Caning Record.

Some might have viewed the disciplinary process at St. Hild's as a little antiquated, in terms of its bureaucracy – never mind in respect of its continuing practice of administering often severe corporal punishment. Girls who incurred the displeasure of the staff for breaches of the countless school rules were issued with a form on which their offences were documented by the offended-against staff member. A pink slip denoted a common-or-garden offence, which would result in a Punishment Detention: an hour in a classroom at the end of the following school day, sitting upright in absolute silence as the giggles of the good girls heading home could be heard from the street outside.

Blue forms were more serious, and their unfortunate (and sometimes deserving) recipients would find themselves in College on the coming Saturday morning, copying out pages of dull textbooks in perfect script, for three whole weary hours. For some reason, a copy of the original eighteenth-century Encyclopaedia Britannica seemed to be a preferred text for such exercises. Why copying reams of material from an outdated textbook should be a sensible use of a girl's time, noone knew. Indeed, perhaps the futility of the exercise was its very rationale.

Yet when Mrs Aston had pulled a green sheet from her desk drawer on that crisp spring Thursday morning, there was but one inevitable outcome. After scolding Miranda for the paper aeroplane that had sailed so gracefully over the bowed heads of the other girls, disrupting the church-like sanctity of the examination hall, she had called the dismayed, panicking girl forward to collect the document that determined her painful fate.

"No, Miss Jobson. I've not had a green slip before, so I won't have a Caning Record."

"Well, my dear, then I'll need to create a new one for you." She pulled out a pre-printed sheet of card, sat down and started filling in the details with her fountain pen. "Miranda Watson. You must be in the Lower Sixth, now, right?"

The girl nodded, palms of her hands nervously, repeatedly smoothing the front of her tartan skirt as the necessary details were added to the form.

"You'll need to take this with you to your housemaster, along with the green slip, and then bring it back once you're finished." No doubt with the details of her recently-suffered punishment neatly inscribed, a permanent testament to the fact that Miranda Watson was now indeed the sort of girl who'd been caned.

--

It couldn't be THAT bad.

Susan D'Arby had been caned last term. She was still alive, still laughing, still happy.

And sweet, cute, kind Katie Young had been punished just a couple of weeks ago, when O'Malley had caught her smoking. She'd been quiet afterwards, but you couldn't tell now if you looked at her.

It couldn't be THAT bad. Surely?

Neither of her classmates had talked much about it, of course. About what actually happened. What is was like. It was as if they'd been admitted to a secret society, whose members protected the mysteries of the ceremony, not a little ashamed of their participation.

Christine James in the Upper Fourth: tall, brash, blonde.... Well, she'd told anyone who'd listen what had happened when she'd been summonsed for swearing at the headmaster, and she'd found a curious audience waiting to be regaled with her tales. Quite shameless: what was there to be proud of, after all? Miranda hadn't joined her throng of listeners: perhaps on reflection she should have been more curious?

It couldn't be THAT bad...?

As Mr Robertson circled behind her...

Couldn't be...

... as she grasped the polished wooden chair legs...

Wouldn't be...

... as she vowed to herself not to cry...

Really...

... trying oh-so-hard not to think what Father would say if he ever (God forbid) found out...

Please don't let it be...

... as she tried to block out the mental image of having had to remove her knickers as her housemaster (ever-the-gentleman) looked discreetly away.

The pain couldn't be worse than the sheer humiliation, surely?

It's an interesting fact that when schoolmasters swap anecdotes about the girls they've punished, as they are occasionally wont to do late at night over a whisky in the common room, there are two schools of thought. Some are impressed by those girls who take their beatings stoically, counting the strokes metronomically as clearly and confidently – nay, even defiantly – as they can, despite the inevitable anguish.

Yet others seem to respect those lasses who are able to give in - for whom the pretence of bravery is a far-distant concept as they sob and murmur their way through the thrashing. So much pluckier, they say, to be able to acknowledge real suffering than to put on a show. So much more honest.

Miranda would have so wanted to be in the former camp, had she known of their tale-telling and debates.

She'd vowed not to show weakness, to protect her pride. Although it couldn't be that bad...

And her resolve had lasted until the fourth of the strokes. Almost all of the way through the apocryphal six of the best.

Four. Doesn't sound many. A minute gone by, maybe: stroke, pause, muttered acknowledgement, pause. Stroke, pause, and on and on.

Surely a young woman could take four strokes without breaking down?

If you're a girl taking the first severe punishment of your young life, the first searing blow fights its way into your soul through a wealth of emotions: curiosity, shame, sheer astonishment.

The second validates the first, yet gives you time to think: to take that conscious decision, to remind yourself of your vow of valour, to grit your teeth and see yourself through the third.

For Miranda, like so many of her predecessors (and, no doubt, like so many girls to follow her in the future), it was the fourth strike that made it unbearable. The pain reached its crescendo; the rattan pressed itself agonisingly across an early stripe; there were still two more to take. And then Mr

Robertson had told her she was doing well, and the tears had started to flow.

Seeing her discomfort, he delivered the last two whacks quickly, and an observer intruding on their private pas de deux would have noticed that these were administered more gently than the earlier strokes. Not that the housemaster was ever minded to cane girls as hard as he might, the first time he punished them.

And he didn't make her dally once it was over: by the time she'd stood up, fragile and tearful, her Caning Record has already been signed, a tissue had been proffered, and he'd commenced his brief supposed-to-be-reassuring, no doubt oft-recited hope-you've-learnt-hope-never-have-to-meet-under-these-circumstances-again speech. The post-punishment formalities scarcely detained her from bursting back into the corridor, from running to the bathrooms, to hide, to allow herself to weep openly, to steady herself and slowly regain her composure.

And twenty minutes later, after she'd dragged herself out to face the curious world – fearing, no doubt, that to lock herself away all day as she wanted to do might provoke another punishment - even Miss Jobson looked sympathetic, as she glanced down at Mr Robertson's neat handwriting on the form, and filed it safely away, never to be seen again.

--

At least, not until the following Monday.

--

It might appear unfair: the other girl's words were at least as wounding as the slap that Miranda administered in response. But it was the slap that brought the Duty Master scurrying across the playground, which occasioned the girl's second green slip so quickly after the first.

If she'd stopped to think, Miranda would have known before she lashed out that it could only have one consequence. That despite the provocation, the teasing about her caning, she should have walked away. That "thou shalt not smite thy fellow pupil" must have been the missing eleventh commandment, so seriously was the offence viewed.

Miss Jobson looked bemused at her request, and not just because of her sheer astonishment that Miranda would have re-offended: "But I can't give you your Caning Record again this soon."

"I don't understand...." Where is it? Let me get it over with. (Let me run away, let it never happen, let the school burn to the ground at this very moment, let the government banish all canes from the kingdom). Give me the form and stop tormenting me...

One week, it transpired. One week that needed to elapse between canings. Hidden away in the rulebook, a buffer zone between beatings. Designed, no doubt, to be protective – girls shouldn't have to take consecutive thrashings. In reality, a cruel blow: three days to wait, to contemplate, to regret. Three nights to run her fingers over her backside as she lay in bed, as if seeking a way to protect it from the indignity that was to come.

A first caning establishes a mutual contract between housemaster and pupil. "A line has been crossed, but it's been dealt with, and we're not going to repeat this." The very ceremony is punishment in itself, perhaps even more than the pain of the blows.

A second caning results from a breach of that agreement. A failure of trust. The rite is by now familiar. The chastisement itself has to compensate.

Miranda had written a letter, before facing Robertson. Late the previous evening, by torchlight, after her father had kissed her goodnight and switched out her bedroom light. After he'd checked that she was OK, noticing an absent-minded, quieter daughter these past few days, and had been suitably reassured that there was nothing amiss.

"I'm genuinely sorry for what I've done, and know it was wrong." Written three times, in fact, before her hands had stopped shaking long enough for her handwriting to be legible; grown-up handwriting, serious, not a little girl's nervous scrawl. A plea for forgiveness. For understanding.

Robertson read it carefully; acknowledged it; folded it, looked up at her standing to attention before him and laid it to one side. "It's a little late for that now."

She knew the routine this time, of course, when he told her to prepare herself. Knew to stuff her knickers in her blazer pocket, to lift up her skirt, to lean "right forward now, young lady."

Knew how much it would hurt. Knew indeed that her once-again-bared backside still ached from the previous week.

But she didn't know how much it would hurt when the rugby-playing gentleman administered a whipping with all his force; couldn't conceive of the extra pain that could be inflicted by the thicker cane that he'd taken from his cupboard as he cautioned her that he'd be making sure that this was her second 'and final' visit to his office, and announced that he'd "be giving her an extra two this time just to make sure."

She was crying before he even started this time. Was she really this sort of girl? The type who end up in trouble on a regular basis? And not just a pink slip girl, a minor villain. The very worst sort of offender.

It was a mere seven days since she had felt how an innocuous little stretch of wood could transform into a fearsome weapon capable of inflicting the most unimaginable pain. Seven days. Almost to the minute.

But she knew as the strokes fell that this was something different. Last week, the strokes landing on her; this week the blows cutting into her. Last week's red stripes: this week's harsh, ridged weals. Last week, her fingers clutching the chair legs; this week, unable to hold her position, and the dispassionate "that one won't count" refrain heard three times as she choked back the tears.

She needed comforting words: "I know you're not a bad girl really". She got "I shall be watching you very closely for any further bad behaviour" and "if there's a next time, I shall be sending you to straight to the headmaster."

And then, just as last week: it was over, and she could start to rebuild her courage to face first Miss Jobson and then her classmates.

Five stars, six stripes

She'd sorted the forms, as usual, into the order he preferred. A girl's profile came first, printed onto yellow paper: date of birth, length of service, department, grade - the very basics of her existence within the hotel hierarchy. Then, neatly attached – with a paper clip, mind, never stapled – came each of the three reports that had occasioned that afternoon's forthcoming encounter. Sorted chronologically, the details of the offence that had led to her first misconduct mark, followed by the second and the fateful third.

He liked the girls' details presented alphabetically by surname, inside a plain blue card folder, which she placed, as always, on the leather surface of the desk in his suite. It was two in the afternoon now; he'd soon be emerging from his weekly conference call with head office, which rarely left him in the best of moods. The girls – four of them this week - were due outside at three. Sharp.

Georgina paused, looking down at the folder. A moment, turning into a minute. The same routine she'd completed every week since her promotion to the post of executive assistant to the general manager of the Royal International Hotel. His 'right hand woman', his 'help in time of need', his 'number one ally', as he described her.

Only there was one difference. For, this week, her own details were recorded within the sheaf of papers.

--

The protocol was clearly explained to all new employees, before they even joined. The selection process was notoriously difficult to navigate: "you only came *second* in the year at your country's top hotel school?", "the hotel at which you currently work wasn't listed in the world's top 100 last year?", "pray why did you take on work experience at a *four* star?"

It was presumably why the Royal garnered such accolades, swept the board at so many awards ceremonies. Take on the very best staff, reward them handsomely, and offer that prestigious line on their résumé which would forever open career doors around the globe.

Oh, that - and the policy of ensuring that any shortcomings in performance were addressed as a matter of the highest priority. Even the tiniest slip was noted, discussed by a line manager, treated as an 'opportunity to learn'. For those in their first three years on the staff, the consequences went further. Should any error be repeated, or be deemed particularly serious, or should the employee's attitude to the problem be insufficiently penitent, then a 'misconduct mark' would be recorded on the hotel's computer system, remaining for a year before expiry.

And every Monday morning, any young lady who had reached her third misconduct mark would receive a letter in her pigeonhole, an ever-so-polite invitation to a 'little discussion' with the general manager that afternoon. Not that she would need to be 'invited', of course: she would have thought of little else in the preceding days. Nor would she dare to decline his offer to meet.

Georgina's fateful conversation had taken place the previous Friday evening, when she'd tidied the papers on her desk before her weekend off, uncovering the handwritten note from a certain Herr Mantz, which had arrived via the head concierge the previous afternoon. A regular guest - favourite suite number 2501, only Gordon's gin with his tonic in the executive lounge - and a member of the Royal's exclusive VIP Club. He'd wished to inform the general manager ("My dear Matthew") of a few "minor irritations" that he'd experienced during his current stay, and "would be grateful to you for a call before I depart for Geneva tomorrow."

Panicking at her forgetfulness, Georgina quickly signed back on to the hotel system, checking Herr Mantz's details.

"Before I depart?" Depart*ed*, already, as she'd immediately feared. He'd checked out early that morning, apparently – according to the front desk manager, who'd seen him leave in the foulest of moods. No doubt he'd been wondering what had been so important as to keep "dear Matthew" from his complaint.

It was therefore with some trepidation that she passed the letter across to the general manager at the end of their afternoon meeting. He'd known how to deal with the situation, naturally. "You should call Bouchard in Geneva and arrange for a couple of bottles – no, make that a case – of vintage Bollinger to be couriered to Herr Mantz's residence this evening, with a note explaining that 'Mr James is so sorry not to have spoken with you before you left this morning, and would welcome your call at any time.'"

"Of course, sir." Trust Matthew – Mr James, as she kept reminding herself she should call him - to know how to calm troubled waters.

He frowned. "And one other thing, Georgina."

"Yes, sir?" She knew already that he would tell her that he was disappointed in her, when disappointing him was the last thing she would ever want to do.

"I am not in the habit of being rude to any of our guests, and the care of our most important visitors is a matter of particular importance to me. You should know that."

"Yes, sir. I do. I don't know what happened. I'm so sorry."

"You will record a misconduct mark on your file before you leave this evening."

But... Her world stopped spinning; a shiver ran down her spine. But... but that would be three. He couldn't seriously mean to...

He'd know, of course, of the one he'd given her two weeks after starting her role in his office: the proofreading errors in his PowerPoint presentation to the World Travel Convention haunted them both to this day. But of her slip in the banqueting department, where she'd worked before joining him - the fine wines placed on each table at the luncheon honouring a particularly stern visiting dignitary from a famously "dry" Middle Eastern state? She doubted that the GM would possibly know that she had been to blame. Although part of her suspected that he just might.

--

As befits a man of his status, Matthew James occupied a rather fabulous villa on the outskirts of town. A former ambassador's home, it was rumoured that the famous designers who'd spent many tens of millions 'refreshing' the hotel itself had found time to 'pop in' and work on their client's home in their 'spare time'. It was too large, of course, for a single man, but status counted when one was in the upper echelons of one's profession, as he often reminded himself during his chauffeur-driven journey home. Even 'at the very summit', perhaps.

Its high-ceiling ballroom echoed with the ghosts of grand dances past. Its library was reputedly the best-stocked in the city, if nineteenth-century manuscripts were your thing. Its lawns, perfectly manicured by a team of gardeners, sloped gently down to the river ablaze with summer blooms. Not unlike the officers' mess in Hereford, he sometimes thought, reflecting back on his former career of which he now rarely spoke, and then only in vague terms and with the utmost discretion.

Despite the delights of 'home', Matthew also kept a suite in the hotel for those evenings when he needed to remain on site. It suited him, too, to be able to make the 'in crowd' feel even more 'in' by inviting them for a glass of something bubbly in his 'private' room.

The suite's living room fitted two armchairs, a sofa and a large desk, with plenty of room to spare. A series of tasteful prints lined the walls; the view from the floor-to-ceiling windows high up on the thirtieth floor never ceased to take one's breath, particularly as night fell over the city's spectacular skyline. The adjoining bedroom was large – the design crisp, modern, some might even say, stern. The bathroom could comfortably have accommodated four junior staff members, had they been relocated from the employee dorms.

He had quickly decided that he preferred the privacy of the suite, rather than the formality of his office, for administering the weekly punishments instituted by his predecessor. The latter was a little cramped, 'room to swing a cat' sorely lacking. He found his Monday afternoon sessions a continuing source of disappointment, yearning for weeks when his team's performance had been so immaculate as to have needed no correction.

He flicked quickly through this week's folder: four visitors, he noted, without taking in their details. Four young women being given the chance to continue their career, when many establishments would simply have dismissed them. That the punishments hurt, he had no doubt; of their efficacy, he was also fully convinced.

His clock struck three; he'd leave them to wait for a few moments. They'd have heard the chimes from the corridor; a few moments would allow them to focus their minds completely on what was to follow. At least today's parade was silent, unlike the notorious incident the previous month when he'd found his three offenders pushing and squabbling in the corridor, fighting over who should be punished first. (He'd thrashed them particularly soundly for their misconduct, naturally, before instructing them to report back to him the following Monday so that he could deal with their original offences).

Finally he opened the door and beckoned the quartet in, making them stand in the small entrance hall.

"Georgina?" sounding puzzled as he noticed his assistant attaching herself to the group.

"Sir." Quietly.

He racked his brains. "Was there something we needed to discuss before I deal with this week's group?"

"No, sir." She bit her lip. "My details are in your folder."

"Ah." Ah, indeed. Ah, and oh dear. He recalled scolding her on Friday and awarding her a mark; after all, it was important to be seen to treat one's own team in the same way as he expected his department heads to treat theirs. That it might be her third hadn't crossed his mind. How unfortunate. He was fond of the girl; she tried hard, worked well, learned fast. How very, very unfortunate.

He remembered the other three, and glanced along the line. Juliet he recognised from the restaurant (three stars, five diamonds). Name badges introduced the others as Alicia, in a smart dress (one of the administrative staff, he guessed) and tearful Petra, described as a 'senior guest relations officer'. ('Receptionist', in lesser establishments, where such a role might not always require such a top-class degree).

He began his well-rehearsed speech: described the Royal's goal of continuing excellence, explained the essential part that the hotel's team played in meeting its very high targets. Noted that they must all be bright, capable, ambitious to have found themselves on the staff. Shared his disappointment at the fact that they were now standing before him in such circumstances. That they had let themselves down.

His quiet, softly-spoken words often took the girls by surprise, had they expected an angry lecture. He left them standing, as he sat back at his desk, reviewing the papers in more detail.

He looked up. None of the girls could bring herself to meet his eye.

And then he asked Petra to step forward.

He flicked through her papers once more. A catalogue of misallocated rooms, the same error repeated three times at the start of the month – the second and third occasions earning her misconduct marks. A sarcastic reply to a guest who'd (perhaps rather cheekily) requested an upgrade, overheard by the duty manager the previous Tuesday. And now – this, as a result.

"I shall offer you a simple choice, as I do with all of the girls who stand in front of me in these sessions, Petra. If you wish to stay in our employ, I'm sure that you understand the punishment that will be forthcoming. If you find that option unpalatable, then we shall dismiss you forthwith from our employ."

"I want to stay, sir." (Of course she did; she loved the place, she was learning so much. She had made so many friends. And the thought of her employment being terminated without reference was too scary to imagine. Even more scary than…)

He caned girls on the bare, with them bent over the side of one of the armchairs reaching out to hold onto the opposite arm. He instructed the trembling girl to lift her skirt and lower her knickers, explained the punishment position, and reached to the top of his bookcase to bring down the dragon cane that served him so well.

The strokes were hard, administered with the long-practised arm of one who learnt his trade as a prefect in one of England's finest public schools. Six strokes, six parallel sets of tramlines across the girl's pale skin. Young Petra's vivid marks suggested that she would be grateful that her role behind reception entailed standing rather than sitting.

And then she stood, dressed, thanked him through her tears, and he made her rejoin the little group.

Juliet's offences combined wrong orders, lost reservations, and a wonderful fiftieth birthday cake delivered to the guest of honour who was celebrating his fortieth. She was a sweet girl: one of his upcoming "starlets", as he liked to call them. Yet starlet or not, the protocol was clear. Her heaving shoulders had as much to do with the fear of what was about to happen, as to the thought she'd had in the corridor as to how disappointed her parents would be if they could see their bright star of a daughter here, now.

She took her whacks remarkably bravely, her polite 'sorry, sir' after each stroke suggesting that she too had shared a higher class of education which had not inured her to the unparalleled pain of a truly sound caning. Repentant before he'd started, inconsolable now, she clutched her backside in evident agony as she walked back to the line.

Alicia came next. She worked in the finance team, he learned, and was studying for her accountancy exams. A graduate recruit: she'd only been with them for four months. And already the complaints regarding inaccurate billing for meetings in the conference wing had proved too much for her manager, who had allocated her three misconduct marks in swift succession over the past fortnight.

Three marks, six strokes, yelps accompanying each so loudly that passing guests in the corridor would be in no doubt as to the general manager's methods. But no matter how plaintively a girl promised that she "won't ever do it again, sir", the fixed tariff of six still stood. Delivered with precision. Hard. Very hard.

And then... He tried to pretend she was just another ordinary girl. Not that any of them were ordinary, of course. Not that for his two minutes with each he didn't invest in her his full attention, his full care, his fullest desire for her to learn her lesson. In a strange way, he reflected, this would take as much bravery from him as it would from her.

Georgina too tried to look brave as she stepped forward. Yet it's hard to look brave, she thought, when you're so terrified. Over the weekend, as she'd cried herself to sleep and cried herself back awake, she'd managed to convince herself that it was her pride that would be hurt the most – to end up here, like this. That was before she'd seen her colleagues take their punishment. Watching the other girls had made her realise that the pain of the caning would be likely to remain clear in her mind long after her pride had healed. This was what daddy had always threatened when he pointed to the willow tree at the bottom of the garden; always threatened, never put into practice.

He spoke softly, but firmly. "The uniform of a member of our hotel management team has to command respect, Georgina. And for our colleagues here to see you wearing it whilst you are being disciplined would undermine that respect. I therefore have to ask you to remove your jacket and skirt, before bending over. And please lean over the *back* of the chair, facing your friends."

Facing her friends, so they could tell from her face that he was not going to be easy on his assistant, his closest helper – perhaps, he might admit, his closest friend. No yielding, no undue leniency. No matter how fond of her he had become over these past few months. How had she ended up here, like this?

She seemed frozen to the spot. So did he.

"Are you waiting for something?"

For the ground to swallow her, for time to warp back four days, for her general manager to remember that exclusion that saved girls in management from the cane? The exclusion that, of course, most certainly did not exist, as a desperate, I-know-this-is-futile search of the staff rulebook had confirmed in the early hours of Saturday morning as the city slept around her.

The back of the chair was much higher than its arms; she was almost on tiptoe as she leaned forward, reaching out to hold the front of the seat cushion. Taut, vulnerable. She glanced up at the other girls; saw their tear-stained faces; full of sympathy – the strange camaraderie that the whipped can offer to the soon-to-be-whipped.

Georgina promised herself to be strong.

Broke her promise on the very first stroke, as she leapt into the air, in shock and sheer agony.

"Perhaps we should start again?"

So he did, whipping her slowly, methodically, allowing just long enough for the pain of each stroke to reach its crescendo, allowing her fingers to clutch the cushion once more, before striping her cruelly with the next. Seven in total, her one extra adding to her shame.

And then it was done, and she was dressing again with shaking hands, avoiding his eyes and resuming her place in the line ready for life to begin again.

The girls held hands, sniffled, whilst the general manager sat at the desk to add a footnote to each misconduct record: his initials and the date, clearly displayed for anyone to see should they ever need to consult the girls' records in the future.

He looked up. "A favour, if I may, Georgina?"

"Yes, sir?"

He held out the folder. "Perhaps you might take this downstairs? Save me a job?" Save him a job; but by making her reappear in the General Office, tear-stained with the notorious folder, sparking endless bouts of curiosity from her colleagues.

And then they were dismissed, with his reassurances and his best wishes for their future. Back to their posts, chastened, corrected, determined to improve, to fix their professional smiles and try to work for the remainder of their shift as if nothing had happened. While Matthew sat for a moment longer at his desk, reaching for the phone to order the bouquet of flowers that young Georgina would find waiting when she returned home to her apartment that night, with its simple message: "To my good girl. From M."

Twenty four of the best

I was quite taken aback at breakfast the other day, whilst glancing through my copy of The Times, to see the headline 'Corporal Punishment to be Abolished'. To be honest, I'd forgotten that it was still actually legal for fee-paying schools in England to beat their pupils.

I can remember the discussion we had when the cane was banned in state schools years ago; although I was teaching in a fee-paying school at the time, we had to stop too, as the law covered girls who were at our college but on government grants under the Assisted Places scheme. It just didn't seem right that we could cane pupils with rich parents, but not those from poorer backgrounds for the same offence!

I was never a fan of using corporal punishment in any case. But the newspaper story got me thinking of the one time I did use the cane - on a girl who's since become one of my closest friends and confidantes.

I guess I ought to give you a bit of background on myself. I'm thirty-nine, the headmaster of a boarding school in South-West England. The events I'm going to relate began eleven years ago - not, as it happens, at this school, but at the one at which I started my teaching career.

I need to go back a bit before that, though, so you understand the reason why the caning, well, *mattered* so much to me. I'd graduated in Economics & Modern Languages from Cambridge in 1980 - with a first-class degree - and then went on to earn my doctorate. During the time I was doing my research, I found myself becoming more and more attracted by the idea of teaching as a career. Needless to say, the money's not brilliant, but education to me is just about the most important thing in life, and I'd got so much out of it that I thought I should try and share some of my learning with others.

So in August 1983, I started work at Winthrop College, a prestigious girls' boarding school. It was a lovely place: an old country house set in open fields in Shropshire, near to the border between England and Wales - so gorgeous that I'd quite fallen in love with it when I went for the interview!

Each girl was allocated to a house when she joined the school - one of six buildings around the estate, with dormitories, study-bedrooms, TV rooms and so on, and each with its own housemaster and tutor - and this element of pastoral care for the girls' wellbeing also impressed me. I settled down very quickly - the teaching was great fun, with classes in Economics for O and A Level, mixed with teaching French to some of the younger girls.

I had been quite concerned about one thing before I started - 400 teenage girls, all boarders, aged from 13-18, stuck in a country house with a group of mainly male teachers. Wasn't there a risk that some of my colleagues might be - well, just a bit, odd? By and large, it didn't turn out to be an issue. Most of the men were happily married, with their wives living with them in the staff accommodation at the school.

There was one thing that did slightly worry me, though, and that was the disciplinary regime at Winthrop. To say it was strict was an understatement: the girls seemed to live in almost constant fear of punishment, and some of the staff seemed to take an almost unhealthy delight in meting out correction. "Arrived two minutes late for a lesson, young girl? Come and bend over my desk at the front of the class and take three swats with the slipper." "Caught misbehaving during the lunch break? Report to your housemaster this evening for six of the best with the tawse."

And worst of all, for those girls committing some particularly heinous crime - the knock on the door in the middle of the lesson, the folded note handed to the teacher to read aloud: "Miss Fisher, would you please go with the headmaster's secretary to his office, as he wants to see you." And fifteen, maybe twenty minutes later, the young lass would knock on the door and come back in, by now dishevelled and with tears in her eyes, and would wince as she lowered herself gingerly into her desk and onto her newly-caned buttocks.

Punishments were a frequent topic of discussion in the staff room as well. The housemasters - who had the main responsibility for the discipline of the girls - would quite often regale the room with accounts of the thrashings they had just doled out: whether they'd used the tawse or the cane, how many strokes they had given, whether the girl cried, and so on. I remember the excitement one morning when a large package marked 'Lochgelly' arrived containing a batch of new 'extra heavy grade' leather tawses, and the vicious two-tailed straps were handed round and much admired. (And I also remember how the housemasters agreed that they would each find an opportunity that day to use the new implements, and then reporting back that evening on the agonies that they had inflicted).

Now, I found it somewhat difficult to relate to all of this. Sure, when I'd been a schoolboy myself, the cane had been used - but not on good boys like me! Here, I guess a girl was lucky if she got through her time at the school without at least one whacking in front of the class. So I passed on using the slipper - and I don't think it had any adverse effects on the discipline that I could maintain with my classes. Far better, to my mind, to trust your students, so that they learn to trust and respect you.

Anyway, my dislike of the disciplinary regime didn't really get too much in the way of my enjoyment of my job. By the end of my second year at the school - in summer 1985 - things were going well for me at Winthrop. The kids I taught seemed to like me - and to get good exam results; I managed to get quite actively involved in various extra-curricular activities (sports, adventure trips, that kind of thing). And even the headmaster, the dreaded Mr Evans (dreaded, that is, by many of the staff, as well as the pupils!) seemed to have taken quite a shine to me.

I went to spend that summer vacation in France. My girlfriend at the time, Marie, was French, and lived in the Loire valley. We'd met whilst I was a student - I'd spent some time in France as part of my course - and I guess it was fair to say she was something of a catch: wonderfully intelligent, stunningly attractive (so much that she turned heads in the street!), and now beginning to establish herself as a successful artist. I look back on that summer very fondly: lazy days, good food and wine and - particularly memorable - making passionate, erotic love to one another whenever (and wherever) the opportunity arose!

It was towards the middle of August that Marie came into the bedroom one morning with the pile of post, and passed me a letter from the school. I was surprised to hear from them - they didn't normally contact staff during the holidays - but its contents were rather interesting. The letter was from Mr Evans, the headmaster, congratulating me on the exam results that had just been published for the classes that I taught, and asking me to "return to Winthrop a day early this autumn and join me for dinner on the night before term starts, as I have a project that I'd like to discuss with you." Intriguing...

So, at the start of September, I drove back over to Shropshire, and found myself eating a splendid meal in the head's private dining room. As dessert arrived, Evans turned the conversation to the project which he had mentioned in his letter. The governors had decided that six houses weren't sufficient to cope with the number of girls in the school, and were starting work to develop a brand-new, purpose-built building to be the seventh house. And then - to my amazement - he offered me the job of housemaster, starting when the new building was completed in twelve months' time.

Frankly, I was astonished. There was I, still in my late twenties - a good ten years younger than any of the other housemasters. He sensed my surprise: "Richard, I wouldn't ask you to do it if I didn't think you could succeed." By the end of dinner, I had agreed - subject to a couple of considerations. Primarily, I wanted his assurance that I would have full flexibility to run the house exactly as I wanted to, and that he would back any decisions that I made. And secondly, I wanted to select a small team of girls straight away, to work with me on deciding how the house should be run. Much to my satisfaction, Evans agreed to both.

"Which girls do you want in your team?" Evans asked. I thought about if for a moment, then listed half-a-dozen names - girls I'd taught, girls with whom I thought I could get on, girls who could make an invaluable contribution to my planning. He nodded; "You want the best, don't you?!" We laughed.

There was only one of the girls on my list that he didn't know: Imogen Jones. I filled him in on her background: aged 15, taking O Levels that summer, quite quiet, a bit shy - but bright, and with that certain something about her that made me think she'd be good on the team. He suddenly remembered her: "She's the lass on the scholarship, isn't she? Parents live in Bristol, he does something for the council?" He was right - although rather typical of Evans to remember her social background; in a school with several aristocrats' daughters, it was actually quite daunting for a girl like Imogen, from a relatively poor background, to fit in.

So, I left dinner that night a happy man, with Evans having agreed to all I had requested. I called 'my girls' together on the second day of term, and asked whether they wanted to be involved - and a more enthusiastic response I couldn't have hoped for.

The next few months were great: the building was taking shape, and the girls and I met regularly to make our plans. Our aim was to make the house the one to which the girls in the school most wanted to belong - not just because of its modern facilities, but more because of its atmosphere and approach. As the year went on, we bonded fairly tightly into a group - helped to an extent by a weekend away in November on a 'team building' event (pretty clichéd, I know, but it worked!). Ideas were exchanged freely and openly, and we began to trust each other pretty much completely; the girls were forever popping into my office to discuss this idea or that.

One of my worries had been that working on the plans might distract the girls from their academic work, but on this count I needn't have worried - they seemed to positively flourish. One of the interesting topics that came up was - not surprisingly - the one of discipline. Rather amazingly, only one of the six had ever been beaten during their time at Winthrop - a girl called Sue, who'd tasted the tawse in her first year. The team desperately wanted me to agree not to use corporal punishment in the new house, and I was minded to accept, given my own thoughts on the matter. So I sent a note to Evans:-

January 27th, 1986

Dear Headmaster,

CORPORAL PUNISHMENT

My team has requested that I agree not to use corporal punishment in the new house. I am sympathetic to this request.

Would you please confirm whether you would be in agreement with such a policy?

Yours sincerely,

Richard Thompson

The reply came back the following day, and I read it to the girls. "I note the comments in your letter to me of yesterday. As you know, I believe corporal punishment serves two vital roles in a school such as ours: as a deterrent, and as a strong punishment for those who do misbehave. If, however, you do not wish to use it in your house, I am prepared to accept that policy, as I have given you the authority to take decisions on how the house should be run. This is, however, subject to your agreement that you would indeed administer such punishment if I were ever to require you to do so in a specific instance."

The girls could hardly believe their luck: the head never interfered in house matters, so the chances of him using his power to override me seemed remote - and a condition worth accepting!

--

By September 1986, the new building was complete, and we moved in, with a full complement of 60 girls. Of the six who had formed my team the year before, two had left to go to university. One of those remaining, Sally, was in the sixth form, and I made her head of house; she immediately asked the other three girls to join her on a 'management team', and the five of us kept to our habit of eating a meal together once a week.

At the first house assembly in September, I explained the philosophy of the new house to the girls. In particular, the discipline issue had to be addressed: "I do not intend to use corporal punishment in this house, ever. I will, however, reserve the right to administer the cane if you put me in a position where I have no choice. If this ever happens, I will be extremely disappointed in you."

Things went well - very well. We started winning just about every inter-house competition that took place; the girls' grades in their academic work all, almost without exception, started to show marked improvements on previous years. And we were having fun!

I took some flack from my colleagues in the staff room about the discipline issue, though. They couldn't understand why I didn't join them in tanning the backsides of my girls at regular intervals - and eventually started to get rather irritable about it. "You give them an easy life." "They'll run rings round you." "They'll take advantage." "Why should my girls get caned for something when yours don't?" (I told them the last of these questions was something they needed to answer themselves, which didn't impress them!).

The only downside for me was the ending of my relationship with Marie. I had less and less time to travel to France, and her work stopped her from getting to Shropshire. In January, she called me, and told me that she had found someone else and was planning to marry him. I was miserable for about a week - so much so that Sally and Imogen, who was in the Lower Sixth by now, bought me a box of chocolates to cheer me up!

--

At the start of the summer term, the headmaster was on the warpath. Just before Easter, there had been a number of incidents of girls getting drunk (none in my house, I'm pleased to say, but the problem was becoming something of a nuisance), and he'd picked up a fair number of complaints from local people.

At our staff meeting on the eve of term, he let it be known that this was something that had to stop, and at the first school assembly of term, he thundered at the girls: "Let me make it very clear that if any of you is caught drinking, you must expect the most severe consequences."

--

As I walked into the staff room the following morning, I was greeted with sarcastic cheers. I wondered why. "What's going on?"

"Haven't you heard?"

"Heard what...?"

"About yesterday's drinking party?"

"No." What was this about, I wondered?

"Well..." Simon Cawthorne, one of the other housemasters, was enjoying this. "You remember Evans' tirade in assembly on the evils of drink?"

"Yes."

"Well seems like a group of our little girlies weren't listening as carefully as they should have been. And our Mr Evans goes for a quiet drink in the pub in the village last night, and who should he find in there knocking the booze back like there's no tomorrow but five of the Lower Sixth." He paused, as if for effect. "Your little Miss Management Team Member Imogen Jones amongst them."

I could hardly believe it. "Imogen?"

"Yes. Imogen. And apparently it's to be sore bottoms all round for them - Evans is writing to each of us this morning with our instructions!"

This was terrible. Im (as she tended to be called) wouldn't do a thing like that.... surely? She was too.... too sensible, too straight. But it sounded very worrying. I didn't know if I could bring myself to punish her, after all the time we'd spent together in the past two years, all the confidences we'd shared, all the trust we'd placed in one another.

The bell rang for the start of lessons. I daydreamed my way through the first three lessons, and wandered up to my office at break. I didn't think I could face the taunts of my colleagues. I felt betrayed, angry.

As I opened the office door, I noticed a stiff, white envelope on the carpet. I picked it up and opened it.

FROM THE HEADMASTER

22nd April 1987

Dear Richard

You will recall my speech in assembly yesterday morning in which I outlined the serious steps that would be taken against any girls found drinking alcohol.

Yesterday evening, I found a group of girls in The Swan public house in Ilfley, all drinking alcohol. I find this clear breach of my instructions extremely annoying, and I am sure that you will also share my concerns at the damage that underage drinking could do to the school's reputation.

One of these girls, Imogen Jones, is a member of your house. I am writing to the housemasters of all of the girls involved, to instruct them to give each offender eight strokes of the cane before the end of today; four for the drinking, and four for their gross disobedience.

I know that I can trust you to deliver this punishment, and look forward to receiving the signed punishment form (attached) by midday tomorrow.

Yours ever,

J. Evans

Eight strokes!!! This was disastrous. I wasn't sure I could bring myself to do this to her. But I had no choice.... I went over to my desk, and scribbled a note. "Imogen. I would like to see you in my study this lunchtime at 1.30pm. Thank you. Richard." As I walked back down into the main school building, I saw one of her classmates, Helen, and passed her the envelope to give to Im as soon as possible. Helen looked at me and smirked - it was obvious she knew what the note was about, and didn't look as if she had much sympathy.

I found it quite hard to concentrate for the rest of the morning, and only nibbled at my lunch. But I did decide on my plan of action - I wouldn't deliver the punishment at lunchtime, but would talk through the situation with the girl, and arrange for her to come back that evening before lights out. It would be better that way: I might not feel so angry with her by then, and at least she would be able to lie on her front for the night rather than having to sit in a classroom all afternoon on her whipped backside.

--

At 1.30pm on the dot, there was a knock at the door. "Come in," I called out.

The door opened slowly, and Imogen entered, white as a sheet.

"Sit down." I pointed to the chair opposite me, across the desk.

She sat, her bottom lip trembling.

"I suppose you know why you're here?"

"Yes." Quiet, almost inaudible. She bit her lip.

"Why did you do it?"

She paused. "I don't know." Her voice was shaky, emotional. "I've been so stupid."

"You can say that again. Read this!"

I passed her Evans' letter. She glanced through it, her hands shaking as she held it. She let out a gasp: "Eight?". She folded the letter over, and passed it back to me. "Are you really going to...?"

"To what?"

"To... to cane me?"

"Why wouldn't I?" I got up, and started to walk around the room, her eyes following me.

"But... but you weren't going to use corporal punishment."

"Not strictly accurate. I wasn't going to use it *unless* I was given no choice. And now I've been given no choice."

"But..."

"No buts."

Tears started to roll down her cheeks. I'm afraid that at that moment, I rather snapped.

"Pull yourself together, girl," I shouted. "How do you think I feel about this? I placed my trust in the girls in this house, and most of all in you, Sally and the others. I care for you - I care for you a great deal. And now this. You've taken advantage of me, Im, and I won't have it."

"It's not like that."

"Well what is it like, then?"

"I made a mistake."

"Yes, you did that all right."

There was silence, for what seemed like an age, but which must only have been seconds. Then I leant over the table towards her, and pronounced my sentence. "Now you listen to me, and you listen to me carefully. I'm going to flog you, Imogen Jones, and I'm going to do it as hard as I can so you learn a lesson you won't forget. You saw the letter: you'll get four strokes of the cane for drinking, and four for disobeying the headmaster. And on top of that, I'm going to give you four more, for betraying my trust in you. So that's twelve in all."

She stared at me, sobbing.

"I'm not going to thrash you now. I want you to go back to your lessons as usual. I want to see you here, tonight, at 10pm, before lights out. Wear your nightie and your dressing gown. Do you understand me?"

"Yes...."

"Any questions?"

"No... I'm sorry!"

"It may be clichéd, Im, but you will be. Now get out of my study."

I turned and looked out of the window. I heard her get up, still sniffing, and heard the door open and shut. And then I went and poured myself a large scotch.

--

I can hardly bring myself to describe the events that followed that evening.

At ten o'clock, there was a gentle knock on the door, and Im walked in, clad in a rather stylish blue and white striped dressing gown, her straight fair hair tied back. Her 18-year old face looked absolutely terrified.

I gestured her to sit down in the chair opposite me. "I won't beat about the bush, Imogen; we both know why we're here, and we might as well get on with it. I'm going to give you 12 strokes of the cane, and then we'll forget all about this. Are you ready?"

"Yes. Yes, sir," she mumbled.

I stood up, and walked over to the cupboard in the corner of the room, and unlocked it. Hanging in there, unused, was the cane that Evans had given me a year before ("just in case"). I picked it out, holding the crooked handle. "Stand up."

"Now, I want you to move the chair out of the way, then bend over and touch your toes, facing the desk." She complied, taking up the position I wanted her in.

But there was something odd. As she bent forward, I could see a bulge under her dressing gown. I tapped her backside with the end of the cane, and found myself tracing round the edges of a rectangular shape. Surely she wouldn't have....?

"Stand up. Turn round and look at me."

She was shaking now.

"What have you got under your dressing gown?"

"My nightie, as you asked for."

"And...?"

"And what?"

"That's what I'm wondering. Take your dressing gown off."

She looked at me, dumb struck, then obeyed.

"Put it over the chair you were sitting on. And then take your nightie off."

"But that's all I've got on."

"Do it."

She reached down, and pulled the nightie up over her head. She held it in front of her, covering herself.

"Put it on the chair." Im did as she was told, then covered her breasts with her hands.

"I see you've got knickers on."

"Yes. But... I always wear knickers in bed."

"Take them off. And give them to me."

"You can't do this."

"I can, and I'm doing so. Get them off."

She bent forward, and pulled the pants down. As she did, my suspicions were confirmed: an exercise book, with cardboard covers, fell out onto the carpet.

"And I suppose you always keep a book down your pyjamas when you go to bed as well, do you?"

"No." She started crying, as she stood up, trying to cover herself from my gaze.

"Put your hands on your head."

She was naked before me, now, totally exposed; her breasts small, firm, the small triangular patch of straight dark pubes contrasting with her fair hair. She was sobbing.

"It's not terribly pleasant, this, is it?"

She shook her head.

I placed the tip of the cane under her chin, and lifted her eyes up to look into mine. "So first you betray my trust by getting yourself into this situation. And now you do it again by trying to cheat me. You are shameful." I was livid. How could she do this to me? She'd pay the consequences, now, for sure.

"I'm sorry."

"Mmm. Well, you give me no option but to give you another six strokes."

"No!" She cried out. "That's eighteen - you can't do that."

"Just you wait and see. Get over and touch your toes. NOW!"

She moved in front of the desk, and bent forward.

"Tighter. Legs straight, touching your toes."

She leaned forward, her pure, fair buttocks rearing up into the air. I measured the cane across its target.

"I'm now going to give you 18 strokes of the cane. You will count the strokes aloud one by one. If you flinch or stand up at any point, the stroke will not count and you'll get an extra one. Do you understand?"

"Yes, sir."

"OK."

And with that, I pulled the cane back above my head, and whipped it down across her arse with an almighty crack.

"Aaaaaaargh." She cried out, panting as the pain built up. The red line stretched straight across the centre of her backside, marking her, the brand of the disobedient schoolgirl.

"Count them."

"One, sir."

I waited about ten seconds. I might not have done this before, but the conversations in the staff room had at least given me some idea of how to maximise the effectiveness of a caning, and rushing it wasn't on the agenda. I wanted her to have time for the pain of each stroke to fully reach its peak.

I smacked the stick down again, just below the first stroke. She caught her breath. "Two, sir."

Then again - this time lower still. "Three, sir."

And the fourth - back between the first two. "Four, sir." By this time the weals on her backside were rising up angrily, four parallel lines of sheer pain.

I brought the fifth down directly on top of the previous stroke, whereupon she jumped up, screeching, clutching her backside. "Doesn't count, Im."

She hopped around, then bent forward again. The next stroke was lower, right along the crease between her buttocks and thighs. Again, she jumped up. She turned to me - "How can you do this to me?". "I could ask the same of you, young lady. Now get down. We're still on four strokes."

She bent forward, slowly, gingerly. She took another five, each separated by a fifteen second gap, and this time managed to stay down between each lash, almost as if we were finding a rhythm, her and me, flogger and flogged. Then on the tenth - actually the twelfth she'd taken, she was up again, dancing around.

"Please stop." She looked me in the eye, pleading with me. I stayed silent, gesturing with the rod to show that she should bend back down. I wasn't going to cave in at this stage, vulnerable as she looked.

Again, she flinched on the next one. "We're still on nine, Im. Half way through. Perhaps you should hold your ankles."

So down she went again. The evenly timed strokes, cracking down on her buttocks like a metronome, the red welts striping her buttocks. "Ten... eleven... twelve... thirteen," and on the next, an anguished cry.

Again, she was standing up, clutching her buttocks in agony. And again she bent down, offering her bruised backside to my lash.

I guess it was a bit cruel of me to put the next stroke directly on top of the previous one, but again it brought her shooting upright. At this rate, we were gong to be there all night.

"Right, my girl. This is getting silly. You've taken thirteen strokes. You've got five to go. Let's get these out of the way. I want you to bend over my desk, and hold onto the other side, tight. And you're not going to let go; you're not going to say anything - don't even worry about counting. You're just going to stay down, and we're going to get this finished. Now: over the desk."

She leant out across the polished surface, her breasts flat against the wood, and grasped the edge. I lined up the stick, lifted it high and whipped it down. And this time I didn't pause: the next stroke followed immediately, directly on top of the previous one. And the next. And the next. And the final one, bringing Imogen screaming to the end of her torment.

"Now get up, and stand in front of the desk."

She staggered upright, as I walked round to my chair, and sat down, opposite her. She clutched her backside.

"We now need to fill in a form, and then you can go. Right, let's work through this..."

--

WINTHROP COLLEGE PUNISHMENT RECORD

Master's name: Richard Thompson

Girl's name: Imogen Jones

Date: 22nd April 1987

Implement used: Senior cane

Strokes allocated: Eighteen

Reason: Drinking (four). Disobeying headmaster (four). Disobeying housemaster (four). Using padding to minimise impact of caning (six)

Additional strokes with reason: Six (flinching)

Clothing worn: None

"And all it needs now is our signatures." I signed it, then offered the pen to the shaking girl, who took it and scrawled her name almost illegibly at the bottom of the page.
"Now get dressed, and get going."
The tears were dripping down her face, as she fumbled for her clothes. She pulled the nightie on, and the dressing gown, and picked up her knickers and the infamous exercise book. She turned and looked at me, blinking away the tears, and then left the room, shutting the door behind her.
It was time for another whisky...

--

The following afternoon - a Saturday, as it happens - I was in my study marking some papers when I heard a knock, and the door swung gently open. It was Imogen. "Can I come in?"

"Sure." We looked at one another as she walked in, slowly - clearly in some discomfort.

"I just wanted to come and say how sorry I am for what happened." And she burst into tears and flung herself into my arms, sobbing.

I held her. "How are you?"

"Sore. It's like - I can't describe it. When you were... flogging me... I mean, I've never felt pain like it."

"You poor lass. I'm sorry - but I did have to do it."

"I know." I gave her a hug. "Thanks for coming to see me."

"I had to. I just had to know whether you hated me now."

"Does it look like I do?"

"No. Thanks."

"OK. Listen, Im, what's happened is over. I meant it yesterday when I said I care for you - this doesn't change anything."

"Thanks. Well, look, I'd better be going." She dried her eyes, and pulled away. "Are we still on for dinner with Sally on Monday?"

"Sure."

"Good - see you later." And then she was gone...

--

POSTSCRIPT

My wife Christine and I are still in touch with Im. She's 27 now, married to Tom, a guy she met at Oxford. She's working as a management consultant in London, and doing really well for herself. We meet up once every two months or so, and she's godmother to our four-year-old son.

But as for that evening back in '87: well, I think that it's best if just the two of us to know about that, don't you?

The punishment cell

They'd left her alone. Here, in this room. Just her and the punishment frame, and the small pile of prison clothes that she'd removed, as instructed, and placed in a neat pile on the floor.

Watson had brought her here. The officer in charge of C Wing. The officer with whom she'd argued earlier in the day. (Why had she argued? Why had she been so stupid? Why couldn't she turn back time?). Led her, handcuffed, down the long, silent, antiseptic corridors, unlocking each of the heavy doors in turn, locking them firmly behind her. Brought the girl who'd questioned his authority to the place where it would be demonstrated to her in such unequivocal terms.

Then left, without so much as a glance.

Ten minutes ago? Thirty? Hard to keep track of time.

Too long. Not long enough.

Her eyes kept glancing to the polished wooden contraption in the centre of the high, bare cell. Glancing, looking away, steeling herself, glancing back. The leather ties that would bind her ankles.

Looking away. Looking away. The smooth, dark wood over which they'd have her bend, the ties for her wrists on the opposite side. Looking away. Looking away.

She shivered and wrapped her arms around herself. It was cold. So cold, sitting here, naked, on this solitary plastic chair. A single bulb hung above her, the only frail source of light or warmth in this lonely place.

She'd been caned on admission, as the magistrate had instructed to her shock and to cries of disbelief from her family and friends crowded into the tiny courtroom. Twenty strokes as she touched her toes in the prison's reception room, between stripping from her own clothes and covering herself with the rough, ugly, government-issue uniform. Each stroke unbearable, for its pain and its shame, each marking her transition, her loss of freedom.

But today was different. No cane here. No mere Admissions Clerk. Any moment now: the prison Punishment Officer, bearing a birch. The birch, of which the girls whispered so reverentially. (Apart, that is, from those who'd received it: they fell silent, looked away, tried not to remember. Tonight, she'd become one of them).

They would flog her until they were confident that she would co-operate fully for the remainder of her sentence, they'd said. Until she understood that girls did not challenge officers. Until she was suitably punished.

Waiting, glancing, waiting.

Crying, softly. Wiping away the tears with the back of her hand.

Waiting, waiting.

And then, in the distance, the sound of a metal door opening and closing, and the clatter of boots on stone growing ever-closer…

The housemaster's secret diary

Thursday, before dinner. Wales.

I have had enough: any more foolishness and I'm going to DEAL with it. Capital 'D', capital 'E', etcetera and suchlike.

I can understand their exuberance. Mountain air (not that Snowdonia really counts as mountains in the overall scheme of things, if pitted against, say, The Alps). Away from the confines of their usual surroundings. A chance to let their hair down.

What does the centre's brochure say again? 'Reach new heights at Carsdale Valley Lodge', or some such nonsense, as if walking up a hill or canoeing across a lake is going to be a life-changing experience.

Perhaps it might be for lasses brought up in some inner-city ghetto ("Now, what's that, Leanne? No, it's not a pig. Yes, go on – good girl, it IS a sheep.") But for this lot? My goodness, half of their fathers own country estates.

Another half are the sort who usually refuse to even contemplate poking the tips of their toes outwith the front door if there's the merest hint of rain in the air ("But dahling, my turquoise cashmere pashmina would be ruined"). And the half who are scholarship girls (if I can be indulged mathematically, there actually being no more halves left to allocate) are probably bright enough to read a map or work out how a compass works without the help of the centre's somewhat thuggish-looking 'activity supervisors'. From glorious military careers slithering in camouflage through dusty deserts and snake-infested swamps, our battle-hardened instructors have graduated to supervising public schoolgirls in the Welsh Mountains. How sad.

It's half term, so perhaps I shouldn't be so concerned? Let my hair, what's left of it, down with theirs. But I am the officially-monikered Responsible Member Of Staff: indeed my new-found title is proclaimed boldly on my bedroom door in the Lodge, as if to remind me of my duties every time I retreat to find a moment's peace and quiet. That's 'Responsible Member Of Staff', shorthand for 'Poor Sod Who Couldn't Avoid The Spring Outdoor Adventure Weekend This Time Having Previously Managed To Do So For Fifteen Years Teaching At St. Hilda's'. Managed to do so remarkable successfully, I must say. Now I know why it's seen as such a poisoned chalice ("A week in the country, Mallon. It'll be good for you. Blow away the cobwebs," as the headmaster had said with a somewhat malicious grin).

My patience almost gave way after tea this evening. Chaos triumphant, the lounge area resembling the aftermath of the Battle of Thermopylae, excepting the lack of dead Spartans, of course. (Perhaps I should title this section of my diary '480BC and all that'?).

Yes, I know they've had an interesting day. I never see the point of abseiling myself – here, let me tie you up and allow you to descend ever-so-slowly and ever-so-safely down the side of the cliff, ensuring that you are in absolutely no danger - lest you graze an elbow or break a fingernail, resulting in the revocation of our safety certificate. Perhaps the being-tied-up part of the equation appealed to some of the girls, I don't know or care.

I sometimes think I'll never know what's really going on inside the dark caverns that pass for the minds of seventeen-year-old girls. Even if I keep teaching them until I am an old and bitter man.

No, I'm not.

Neither old, nor bitter.

Really. I'm not.

Thursday, later. Still in Wales (unfortunately)

Too much later. When I should be curled up in bed, with Mr Trollope for company. Not reflecting on a sorry tale of a broken window, an irate Centre Manager ("we'll have to charge you", as if a fifty-pound glazier's bill is going to bankrupt St. Hilda's), and a ghost. It has to have been a ghost that broke the window. None of the girls was anywhere near it, or so they assure me, so adamantly that it would be funny were it not so pathetic.

I should have thrashed the lot of them until a confession was forthcoming.

I probably would have done, had it been term-time in Buckinghamshire, not half-term in North Wales.

And a few of them – the ones in my house - know that; a couple of them have been on the less comfortable end of my cane in the past. Jennifer was looking quite nervous, for example, as it clearly didn't require too much of a memory feat for her to realise that I wasn't issuing idle threats when I reminded them that I was acting on behalf of ALL of their housemasters whilst we were away, and was invested with FULL authority in every respect.

Including discipline.

And that I did have a cane with me.

Just in case.

For a quiet girl, Jenny took it very bravely when she visited me for her painful little encounter in my study last term, as I recall. Very bravely. I'd have expected her to howl the school down.

Then again, had it been term-time in Bucks, the window would doubtless have remained pristine and unadulterated. I never thought I'd yearn so for the comparative order of the school campus.

Final warnings, dire consequences, and so on and so forth have echoed round the Lodge.

Friday tomorrow. Raft building. Oh, how very boy scouts. Girl guides, with this lot, I guess. Then Saturday and the 'grand trek' through the deepest, darkest, most remote forests to be found within three hundred yards of the main trunk road. Then Sunday, and back to the blissful peace and quiet of St. Hilda's.

Oh, for Monday morning. A Lower Sixth discussion on Marlowe, then forty minutes quizzing Victoria on Blake before her interview at Cambridge. Will she loathe him as much as I do, I wonder? I'd quite forgotten that my favourite scholar and I had caught ten minutes yesterday, whilst dinner was being prepared: which particular mills had he had in mind, she'd wondered, and quite how dark and satanic had they been? ("Oh, scarily dark. Diabolically so, I should imagine.") Bright, fun, sharp, inquisitive: I wish the other girls on the trip were of a similar ilk.

I must sound like one of the first-year girls, ticking off the days on the calendar hidden in the top drawer of her bedside table.

Friday. 11.45pm. Wales. Get me out of here.

Well, I've just whipped the three girls in the room above mine, and the noises levels have diminished accordingly to a bearable level.

I'm told it was Mark Twain who wrote that, "Common sense isn't all that common." He could have had the Misses Jardine, Ellis and Walsingham in mind at the time. Good grief, how foolish must they be? Exam question: "It's after lights out and RMoS [Responsible Member of Staff] is trying to sleep in the bedroom directly below you. Do you (a) get into your beds quietly, or (b) invite a friend around, crack open the bottle of premium vodka and switch on a CD player at full blast?"

They, of course (being Fiona Jardine and Amanda Ellis) went for option (b), welcoming in Elizabeth Walsingham who'd sneaked along the corridor from her own room. Wrong option. Definitely the wrong option.

I wasn't in the best of moods, to be frank. The raft-building day had been a nightmare from start to finish, exuberant girls lashing their own Titanics together from oil barrels and rope, and racing them towards the centre of the lake before they sank to its deepest reaches. Deepest being about waist-deep, I should add. Over-exuberant, muddy, wet girls traipsing around the Lodge all evening until I ordered some of them at cane-point to go and shower.

And then a barbeque ("would you care for the under-cooked chicken or the cremated sausages, Mr Mallon?") without – obviously – even a glass of red to wash it down. Perhaps I should have asked the girls: the stashes in their wardrobes presumably resembled the fine wine department at Fortnum's.

I know some of my colleagues have tolerated late-night fun and games in previous years, but the 11pm lights out rule has been written on a tablet of stone throughout the past week. That still gives them an hour more than on a normal school night, and I honestly don't see why pupils should be revelling until two in the morning.

Except, as I say, that my friends from upstairs had better ideas.

The changing palette of emotions displayed on their young faces in the seconds after I opened their door, cane in hand, was quite remarkable to observe: panic, shock, disbelief, denial, horror, embarrassment, shame, nervousness, fear. Drunken giggles quickly subsided into terrified, stone-cold-sober silence.

Fiona was trying to hide the bottle behind her back. An elfin thing: slightly untidy, quick-witted, sharp enough to land in trouble on a none too irregular basis. Good hockey player, mind you.

"It's only water, sir." Pitiful. I expressed surprise that the Welsh sold their water in Russian bottles, and drained it down the sink in the corner of the room.

"We didn't mean to disturb you, sir." Elizabeth leapt to their mutual defence. One of Malcolm Watson's house. Nice girl: I'd taught her for a couple of years when she'd been 14, 15. Much-respected. A candidate for the prefecture, come the discussions in a few weeks' time, I would say. Winner of this particular evening's prize for stating the obvious. (Oh for a frank, "Sir, we decided we wanted to have some fun and gambled that we'd get away with it.")

And then Amanda. Silent in the corner. Amanda. One of the banes of my life when she'd joined the school – her "I don't like it here" passing through "I'm going to be un-co-operative" into "I'm going to be rebellious" and straight into my study for three? four? canings of increasing length and severity in as many terms. Swearing at an opposing teacher on the lacrosse field had led me to despatch her to the headmaster's office, whither she'd returned very meek, immaculately behaved and impeccably compliant.

"I assume that you were all partaking in the Russian... water?"

Sensible girls, to nod so honestly.

I let them stand in silence for a moment, before firing off carefully-memorised bullets from The St. Hilda's Code of Conduct.

"Breaching lights out: one to four strokes. Possession or consumption of alcohol: two to four strokes. Supplying alcohol to other pupils: four to eight strokes." I could see the potential tallies totalling in their eyes as if on old-fashioned cash registers – *caning* registers? Old-fashioned, gently swaying, slightly drunken cash registers.

I looked at Elizabeth. "Is this your room, Miss Walsingham?"

"No, sir." As I well knew.

"Then I shall take that into account. Did *you* bring the vodka?"

Trembling in front of me, poor thing. Tongue-tied. I knew the routine of this long-standing puzzle. With no chance of the punishment being waived, the best case was that one member of the group would be caned; worst case, they'd all be for it, with extra for disobedience. If it were true, she'd therefore own up immediately – she knew she'd be whacked, and honesty might minimise the tally; rare the girl whose cowardice or cruelty would inflict unnecessary suffering on her co-accused.

Were it false, she might still own up to protect a more fragile friend. A noble act of self-sacrifice, but in practice unusual. Yet naming the guilty party would breach the code d'honneur: a betrayal unlikely to be forgiven, whatever the truth of the matter.

Silence, therefore, most likely equalled innocence.

Elizabeth remained silent.

As did I.

I swear I could see the wallpaper craning forward to hear what would come next.

"I brought it with me from home, sir." Fiona.

"Thank you for your honesty, Miss Ellis."

I looked around: there was just enough space for a satisfactory swing if the girls bent over the end of the table that was pushed against the right-hand wall of the room. I gestured Amanda into position, spectres of her younger self whisping between us.

I noticed her friends reach for each other's hands. I let it pass.

"One for lights out. Two for drinking. I'm sure the minimum punishment in each case will have sufficient effect."

I measured the cane across her pyjama bottoms: scant protection. And drove home her lesson, three sharp strokes in quick succession. She whimpered; she was remembering far more than these three whacks.

"Change places with Miss Walsingham, please." Amanda stood up, sniffing, shaking, as Elizabeth replaced her across the desk, trying to look confident.

"Two again for drinking, but two for lights out, as you were out of your own room." Had she been caned before? I doubted it before I inflicted the first cut; her tears by the third suggested not. A valiant attempt to regain self-composure saw her through her fourth and final stroke, before Fiona Ellis stepped up to the block, draping herself into position.

"One lights out. Four for supplying the drink. It hardly seems fair to add more for drinking it too." Five hard whacks is enough to subdue any girl. Her wriggling protests nearly earned her more, but I was erring on the side of generosity. Fiona's muttered "Thank you" was barely audible as she rejoined her friends.

And then I left them to it. I gave Elizabeth five minutes to get back to her room: I guessed they'd want to comfort, commiserate, console and cry, and it scarcely seemed fair to exclude her from her friends' arms.

So now I'm back in the comfort of my own bed, with twenty pages to go before I'm done with 'The Warden' for at least the fourth time. The cane is recovering, back in its case. And all I can hear around me is pure, unbroken, blissful silence.

Sunday evening. St. Hilda's (at last).

Madness. Sheer madness. Statements to the police until eleven last night. Profuse apologies to the Centre staff and the mountain rescue team (whose dogs, at least, seemed to have had fun). Adamant refusal to speak to the Snowdonia Weekly News, or whichever rag the snail-like reporter defaced with his measly prose.

I could picture the headlines now: "Posh girls' booze-up causes mountain chaos", or some such nonsense.

Actually, come to think of it, that would probably be a reasonable enough title.

I don't want to write about it. Really, I don't. Don't want to think about it again. Anyway, I've relived it enough whilst persuading various youthful constables and slightly-less-junior officers that ours was a most eminent establishment that really wouldn't dream of "wasting police time". Particularly, as the headmaster had asked me to point out, since their Chief Constable's own wife was a former pupil and on the Board of The Old Hildonians.

Funnily, the girls scarcely mentioned the day's events on the long coach journey back to school this morning. They must want to erase the memory too, although tomorrow morning may inhibit them in that particular aim.

I actually blame the centre for arranging a trekking route on the final day that went so close to civilisation. If they'd dropped the girls on a remote hillside – left them on Glyder Fawr or some other such scary peak and made them walk carefully down – then temptation would have been well out of their reach. Better still, drop them at the foot of the mountain, make them walk up and tire them out completely. Sending them on a meandering stroll that took in a succession of local villages on an unusually warm late March day was asking for trouble – even if the group had started out unusually quiet given the previous evening's occurrences, of which word had spread like the plague through medieval London.

Not that my three miscreants from the night before didn't behave impeccably, as you might imagine. Fiona came over after breakfast and apologised; a friendly hand on Elizabeth's shoulder reassured her; a quiet stroll with Amanda, away from curious ears, established that she would be fine.

So, in brief, and for the record. We set the girls off in teams of four: maps, compasses and Kendal Mint Cake to hand. Five teams duly arrived home, tired but happy, at around three-thirty.

The sixth group was nowhere to be found. Their mobile phones – not that such infernal devices work too consistently when surrounded by three thousand feet of bulking mountain – were switched off.

Ex-SAS types from the centre's staff scattered to all corners of the route, lest bodies were strewn at the foot of some long-abandoned quarry. The headmaster was phoned. Parents informed. Panicking girls back at the centre reassured to the best of my ability.

And yes, by six thirty, the mountain rescue helicopter did take to the air. But at least I can say, hand on heart, that not too much time or fuel was wasted, as our absentees walked nonchalantly through the door just as the Search and Rescue team was leaving to hover above the valleys. "What's going on? Is there a problem?" Such an enlightened question, from such a doomed group.

I began to wonder what some of these former soldiers had actually done in their military lives, such was the ferocity of the inquisition that followed. They'd stopped in a pub. For a 'lemonade'. Poppy's ankle had been hurting; they'd needed to sit down. Harriet, Libby, Francesca hadn't wanted to leave her there on her own. They'd forgotten the time. Miscalculated how long it would take to get back to the centre.

"Have we really caused all this trouble?"

I didn't cane them: He (and at times like this, our beloved headmaster merits a god-like capital 'H') insisted that matters should be left to Him, after He'd spoken "at quite considerable length to each set of parents about the measures that I intend to take."

I have no doubt that tomorrow morning will see the quartet being flogged in assembly, his favoured method of dealing with the most serious once-every-three-years type of offences. Prefaced by the usual Monday morning melange of hymns, readings and announcements, whilst the guilty parties stood in dread amongst their contemporaries, contemplating their fates. And then up they would be called onto the rostrum at the front of the hall, to be lectured in full view on the severity of their offence and on the corresponding severity of their impending punishment.

Then one by one, into the centre of the stage. Told to face away from the audience. The order to lower their knickers and bend over; their skirts lifted clear, baring them to public view.

His thickest senior cane. Twelve strokes of an intensity that makes my hardest blows look like gentle taps. A tearful, painful stumble back to the side of the stage. And then the next in line made to step forward for her three minutes of anguish.

And then we'll be back to normal. Even the whipped girls won't be allowed a respite: five minutes from trooping out of the assembly hall, they'll be seated in excruciating agony on our ancient wooden benches, alongside their classmates, pretending that they're able to pay attention to the first lesson of the day.

I never want to see Wales again.

Bring on the Lower Sixth. Bring on Marlowe.

Bring on Victoria. Bring on Blake.

From left to right

To each girl, a number. No names, from here on. One to six, read out, the order decreed by the sheet of paper pinned to the top of the punishment officer's clipboard. No need for differentiation. The offences that had brought them to this point, here, in this narrow corridor, were almost irrelevant now. All they had in common was their sentence: today's was a fifty-stroke parade.

"Line up in order!' A scrambling, as girls half pushed, half politely-stood-aside-lest-they-were-being-watched.

And then the cold instruction to strip, in the officer's clear, clipped voice. Some had felt the nudity to be unnecessary, when the law had been before parliament. Its proposers had been adamant: anything that might offer a clue as to origin, class, wealth was unacceptable. 'Equality of punishment for all', they insisted resolutely.

Hands trembling, the girls complied. The more sensible of them had worn T-shirts, jogging pants, slip-on shoes. The wiser; the ones who'd done their research; the ones who'd dared to anticipate what it might actually be like. The terrified fair-haired lass at the end struggled with the buttons of her well-pressed designer blouse, regretting her choice in the same way her neighbour's choice of snugly-fitted trousers would later seem profoundly ill-advised.

They laid their clothes behind them on the narrow bench. Neatly. Trying - far, far too late, of course - to make a good impression.

"Face the front. Hands by your sides." The officer walked along the trembling queue, as if inspecting a guard of honour. Bared girls suppressed their reflexes - resisting the temptation to cover themselves from his penetrating gaze. He paused, allowing them a final moment in the anti-chamber; a final respite before the inevitable. And then he pushed at the door: "Follow me in silence, and line up in order once you are inside."

The bright lights of the punishment room took them by surprise after the dimly-lit corridor. The same smell of municipal disinfectant perfumed the air. High-ceiling. Windowless. Locked away from the rest of the world.

Waiting for them: two guards, wearing the blue uniform of the State Judiciary. One at each end of the room. Tall, thick-set. The sort of men who could, would whip girls until they sobbed, without a moment's hesitation.

And also waiting, the six punishment blocks, evenly spaced. Crafted from oak, to the government specification: in the shape of an upturned U, bolted firmly to the floor. Adjustable, so that each offender was positioned at precisely the right height: the details on their forms had been noted, their punishment positions carefully prepared to await their arrival.

A terrified girl waited behind each. Two weeks, more, since their court appearances: the moment they had been dreading since they'd heard the magistrate's words. The moment when their hopes had vanished, their fears had come true, when he'd informed them that they were to be flogged. The moment that optimistic friends, family had assured them on the way into the courtroom would not be theirs.

"Step forward. Lean over the bench. Hold on at the front."

Instant obedience, stretching forward into the uncompromising position.

The punishment officer walked behind them, pushing legs apart with his feet, reaching down and securing ankles tightly with leather straps. He turned and strolled back along the front of the line, taking wrists, pulling hands downwards until they clenched the foot of the frames: tightening their positions.

He stepped forward, surveying the line. "You have each been sentenced to fifty strokes of the cane. You will remain in position throughout. Failure to comply may result, at my discretion, in you being brought back here at a later date for further punishment." He paused, allowing them to soak up the importance of compliance, lest they were in any doubt. And then he gave the order: "Guards: please begin."

The girls at either extreme suffered first: numbers one and six, howling through the lashes. Rhythmically, systematically, in unison the guards then marked the court's displeasure from opposite ends of the line. One right-handed: the other left. Symmetrical, almost. Pausing between strokes; lifting the cane high; sparing no energy.

"Eight, nine, ten." Hardly started, really: for all the obvious anguish, not yet even beginning to approach the severe punishment that the magistrate had decreed them to deserve.

The punishment officer kept count, as if taking pleasure in each excruciating blow. One cut, three, would have sufficed to send these girls home punished enough never to darken the court's portals again. But one, three would not have punished sufficiently, nor deterred other potential offenders.

"Thirteen, fourteen, fifteen." Girl one seemed resigned to her fate: wailing, apologising, Girl six begged for forgiveness. None was forthcoming. As she must have known.

Girl two was sobbing too, the squirming reactions of her thrashed neighbour confirming her own worst fears.

"Nineteen, twenty, twenty-one." The other girls, bent over, were now resolutely staring at the floor in front of them. They'd looked round, of course, at the start. Assessed what would soon be theirs: tried to calculate the pain from the height of the rod before it descended, the look on the faces of the punisher and punishee. Assessed, then tried to forget immediately. Tried, failed, as every stroke fell, as it would on their own backsides within minutes.

"Twenty-three, twenty-four, twenty-five. STOP! NEXT OFFENDER!"

But... But... The two flogged girls' relief at the unexpected respite was tempered with confusion. "But I've been sentenced to fifty" - unspoken, of course. Blended with a flash of the wildly optimistic: "Have they forgotten?" Mixed with the sheer panic of the next two offenders, their minutes-away floggings now entirely imminent.

Girls two and five. The same procedure. The guards stepping one place inside, nearer to the centre of the line. The same merciless severity, doing the court's cruel bidding. The same howls of all-too-late repentance. The same red stripes, criss-crossing pale skin. The same weals rising up.

And the punishment officer counted, and the rods lifted high, and the blows fell.

"Ten."

"Fifteen." Fighting the pain, trying to kick out as the strokes landed; the leather around their ankles holding them tightly in place.

"Twenty," as girls three and four tensed: counting down, as their compatriots still counted up to the "Twenty-five", their merciful release.

A pause. The guards stood close now. Face-to-face. A momentary glance: a meeting of eyes. Right hand, left hand, raised. Cracked down, so hard, girls three and four now bearing their first stripe, their second line, their third angry weal, their first sobs and cries and pleas for forgiveness.

"Ten." The point at which the flogging started to become unbearable. But for the other four girls, the time for their breaths to start to calm, to become more even: the pain, still excruciating, but crescendoing no more.

"Fifteen." Almost over, for the majority of the girls. Yet the cruellest lashes just starting for the middle two.

"Twenty," adding up one-by-painful-one to the twenty-fifth and the instruction to the guards to desist. They turned, paused, walked to the back of the room, out of sight of the girls. Silence descended, as even the final two victims tried to control their bawling.

The punishment officer, compere, conductor, walked along the front of the line. Looked down, lifted faces with his hand, admired the job well done.

Waited.

Moved over to the front of the room once more. Picked up his clipboard. "NEXT OFFENDER!"

And the guards swapped sides, the cruel logic of the punishment becoming clear. Back-to-back now, they positioned themselves, before numbers three and four felt the harsh impact of their calculations: "Twenty-six", with the tip landing on the opposite side to its twenty-five predecessors, "Twenty-seven" continuing to plot out the mirror-image, "Twenty-eight", "Twenty-nine", as the court's anger at their offences started to move to an entirely different plane.

And girls one and six sobbed openly. The brave ones who'd gone first. The ones whose hopes had been lifted. The ones who had to wait...

"Fifty" done, and the guards paused. That two of the girls could draw breath, were over, had completed their tally, was hardly noticeable: the pain of the whipping was too severe, almost, for them to comprehend anything other than the searing, merging lines that burnt across their backsides.

And, in any case, girls two and five were now squealing, screaming their way to their stark half-century. Vows to be good, prayers to their gods, promises to their guards: there was no magic spell, no easing of the metronome, no lessening of the ever-increasing pain.

"Fifty." A pause. The guards walked back to the rear of the room once again, delaying the already-delayed finale for girls one and six. The two men mopped their brows, then picked up their canes and marched back into position, the next blows falling almost as soon as they had arrived behind their tied victims.

Only two batches: twelve plus thirteen. Five lots of five: I can do that. Count down, do the maths, concentrate on the numbers, getting lower all the time. Blank one's mind. Cry every fifth stroke. It'll be almost done once they get to thirty. Every scheme, every calculation that the first, final girls had mentally computed as they'd waited, worth nothing as each individual lash cut in.

"Thirty."
"Thirty-five."
"Forty."
"Forty-five."

Drawn out. Taking forever. A countdown, finally, as the punishment officer counted up to the moment of release.

"Fifty."

Done.

Six girls united. Punished girls. Beaten girls, released one by one from their leather restraints, reaching back to touch their whipped behinds then reaching forward again sharply, that touch too agonising to bear.

Six girls who would never see one another again. From good homes, devastated parents waiting outside to pick up the pieces. From broken homes, arriving alone and leaving even more so. Intelligent, with degree certificates proudly mounted on family walls; girls who'd struggled even to read the evidence against them.

Six girls, punished equally: justice, such as it was decreed, duly done. Left hand, whip: right hand, whip, all the way to the repentance that the magistrates had required.

The sequence of events

There's that frisson at the very moment you commit the offence - knowing the consequences, choosing to ignore them, so caught up in the daring and the excitement that you're quite blasé about the chances of being caught. Invincible. Invulnerable.

There's the quickened heartbeat as you learn - hours later - that the offence has been discovered. You overhear a comment in the classroom; edge closer to hear the conversation; try not to blush or look guilty.

There's the sleepless night in the dorm. "But surely they won't be able to trace it to *me*? Will they....?" And the recurrent images of what would happen were you caught, painted so vividly into your imagination – a collage of the snippets shared by girls who'd tearfully described what it had been like.

There's the instant at the house meeting the next morning when you hear your name read out. Out of context, at a moment when hearing your name can only mean one thing: "I'd like to see you in my study after lunch." When every head turns towards you, in shock and astonishment.

There's the wait. The long wait. The longest morning ever.

There are those comments in the playground at morning break; the sympathetic hugs almost harder to bear than the occasional barbed tease.

There's the moment in that geography lesson when you finally bury yourself into a textbook: lost in study, absorbed in the topic, only for the thought of what's to come to creep back into your consciousness, unwelcome, overwhelming.

There's the bell at the end of morning school. Lunchtime! *That* time, the ringing celebrating not the usual spell of freedom, but the imminent execution of the sentence. You stand, dreading what sitting back down on that hard desk seat will be like in an hour's time. You reach, subconsciously, to cover your bottom.

There's the food before you in the school canteen. Pushed around your plate. Returned, uneaten, for who could have an appetite?

There's the sight of your housemaster, sitting at the high table at lunch, frowning, deep in discussion: about you?

There are the eyes of the whole school on you as you leave the table: word travels fast when a girl's for the whack. And the arms of your best friends, hugging and encouraging and ruffling your hair, when all you want is to be alone.

There's the moment when you walk straight past the common room, rather than turning in as you usually would to relax, to make coffee, to gossip. Oh, they'd be gossiping this lunchtime, alright, and you knew what about.

There's the green wooden door, leading from the quadrangle to the corridor lined with the housemasters' studies. The steep, scuffed stairs: you pause, scarcely able to bring yourself to climb the mountain before you.

There's the pounding of your heart as you reach the summit.

There's another girl, from the year above you, already waiting before you in line. You'd thought you'd be the only one: now the two of you have to wait together, silently united in your shared dread of your mutual, solitary fates. You notice that she's trembling; you realise that you are, too. You stand, straight, not daring to slouch, in your private universe isolated from the rest of the school.

There's the wait. The housemasterial coffee must be taking a long time to drink on that high table. ("Why did I do it? Why did I get caught?")

There are footsteps on the stairs that lead up from the common room to the other end of the corridor... Drawing nearer... A black gown, sweeping towards you... He passes you, unlocking the study door.

--

There's the other girl's name, spoken firmly: "You'd better come in, as you're first in line."

There's the silence. You press your ear to the door, faintly hearing the voices inside, then step back smartly lest he opens it and catches you.

A long, long silence.

A sudden crack.

And the sob, audible through the door.

The pause. Silence again.

The second stroke, louder. How many would she get?

A cry.

The third, following quickly on.

There's silence once more. And then the door is opening, and she's emerging into the corridor, tears in her eyes.

"He asked me to send you straight in." And the late-remembered, quietly-murmured, "Good luck!"

There's the crisp instruction. "Stand up straight in front of my desk." And the lecture: surprise, concern, disappointment ("especially for a girl like you").

There's still the faint hope of reprieve - your past good conduct to be taken in mitigation, your apologies (profound, oh-so-genuine) to be heard. The flickering candle of hope extinguished with, "I'm glad that you appreciate the gravity of your misconduct. Indeed, it's precisely because you breached the school rules so seriously that I've called you into my study for punishment."

There's the moment when your worst fears are confirmed. "I have no choice but to cane you." And the dread news, that you must have expected, that you'd be receiving six strokes. No reprieve here from the full tally. You'd hoped, of course, but you'd known, deep down.

There's your first sight of the cane, taken from the top of a bookcase. Flexed, ominously. So long! So whippy! (Anything but this...)

There follow the instructions that you knew from the other girls, who'd preceded you into this and other studies: "Lift up your skirt, and touch your toes." You'd rehearsed the moment mentally; this was the real performance.

There's the final part of the traditional choreography: "Your caning will be on the bare. Please reach back and lower your knickers. And count the strokes as we go through."

There's your imagination, in overdrive now as you wait in position, staring down at the carpet, wondering when it will start, dreading what it will be like.

There's the sudden sensation of the rod across your backside. Touching lightly. You realise that your housemaster is measuring the stroke, deciding where it should land, preparing for it to start...

--

You know, after you've been through all of that, the moment when I draw back the cane and lift it high into the air is almost incidental.

I bring it down hard, flicking my wrist at the last moment to cut it across you with the maximum impact. I leave the rod there momentarily, knowing that the force of the stroke will have shocked you. And then I remove it, stand back, watch the white stripe take colour as the weal raises up, knowing that the pain will be building inexorably.

I wait for you to count the stroke. Remind you, as you're lost in the agony of the stroke just received and the terror of five still to come. Have the other girls told you that I cane harder with each successive stroke, I wonder?

And then you compose yourself enough for me to measure you again, and crack down the second, perfectly parallel to the opener. It draws a yelp; composure is longer coming this time.

I punish you. I demonstrate the school's disapproval of your reckless misconduct. *My* disapproval.

Three. Harder, lifting you onto your tiptoes, rocking you forward. Your count sobbed out this time, as you thank me for the excruciating stroke.

You're a good girl. That much I know, after the nearly four years you've spent in my house. What on earth possessed you to blot your copybook, to be so foolish – to incur *this*?

I raise the rattan higher this time. Pause, watch you waiting. Slice it through the air, cutting home hard. You hold position for a moment, then reach back, clutch your behind.

I choose to be lenient. I could re-apply the stroke, of course. With some girls, I would. You don't need me to: the punishment set out in the school rules (approved by the governing body, kept in a leather volume for all to consult in the library) is quite sufficient to assure us both that you won't return.

The next laid with full force along the line of the first. Tears flowing freely now: "Five, thank you, sir." You're a brave girl. Taking it well. I've seen hardened pupils, here for their third, fourth caning take their floggings with much less dignity.

And then I wait, allowing you to compose yourself; waiting for you to be still; giving you time to contemplate, permitting you to realise that your thrashing is almost through, pausing until we are both ready.

I step back slightly. Flick the air with the cane, then cut it across you. The final stroke, traditionally the most severe: no exception here. You rise upright, hands darting instinctively to clutch, to try to soothe.

You realise that I'm waiting. "Six, sir. Thank you. Thank you, sir."

"Turn around."

You face me, your skirt falling back into position to cover you. I know, you know, that that final stroke should not be allowed to count. I tap the cane against the outside of my leg.

"Please don't, sir…"

I pause. I glance up at the clock on the wall, then back at you.

"Tidy up your uniform - and go and wash your face before the next lesson." I prop the cane against my desk, and brush past you to open the door.

"Yes, sir. I'm sorry, sir. It won't happen again."

But I know that already. You'll wash your face, then hide, then creep into class at the last moment, evading the other girls' stares and biting your lip as you sit down. You'll try and concentrate through the pain, read your books through misty eyes.

And I'll set off to *my* next lesson, and continue my quest to inspire twenty-five girls with a lifelong love of Latin. By the time I next see you - on the way into dinner - you'll be smiling weakly and trying to join in the banter once more, and I'll give you a reassuring squeeze on the shoulder as I walk past towards the high table...

The colonials

"I'm so sorry, sir. I wasn't looking where I was going." The giggling girl smoothed down her skirt and straightened her dark blue blazer, before starting to brush at the sleeve of his dark, expensive pin-striped suit. Her friends scurried around on the floor, gathering the important-looking papers that had scattered across the pavement.

The gentleman carefully, firmly removed her hand from his sleeve. "Stop pawing at me, girl. And I'd like an explanation as to exactly what you were playing at."

"It was an accident, sir. I'm sorry," she responded, with a gaiety in her voice that didn't smack of the greatest degree of regret. The girl's friends behind her sniggered just too loudly. She herself pursed her lips, trying not to smile. He did look rather serious and self-important after all, and the gentleman's two burly companions hardly looked the most friendly or humorous of kinds. "Sorry, sir," she muttered once again, suppressing more laughter, and turned away.

"Not so fast." The gentleman caught her by the arm this time, and spun her round to face him. Sternly, he informed her, "I want to talk to you."

"Let go. You're hurting me." She drew back, towards the shade of the sun-blazed trees.

"Don't tell me what to do." He tightened his grasp on her arm, his pale blue eyes staring into hers. He was quite handsome, she supposed, if you were into fifty-year-old men. Craggy, athletic. Real presence. Scary.

"I'll call the police if you don't let go." Behind the bravado and the idle threats (where would she find a policeman, and what precisely would she say?), a mild sense of panic was creeping into her voice now as she looked him up and down. Her friends were drifting backwards, fading into the thin shadows, as if planning their escape.

He smiled and released his grip, gesturing to his two partners. "I shouldn't worry: there are two of them here. Quite senior members of the constabulary, as it happens." It was his turn to smile now - but a smile as cold as ice. "So would you like to press charges?"

"No, sir. Please. Let's leave it. I'm sorry I bumped into you." She stepped out of his reach. "Have a nice day and all that."

"Wait there." It was clear from his voice that he didn't expect her to disobey. "The Convent School, am I correct?"

"Yes, sir."

"Mmmm. I recognised the uniform. My daughter has just started. Miss McPherson has been so helpful and considerate."

The headmistress. Dreaded. Feared. Respected.

But who was his daughter?

"Yes, sir."

"So I can't help to ask myself what Miss McPherson might say if I told her that a group of her girls were darting around the street in the middle of the school day, crashing into people at random and making a nuisance of themselves?"

The lass tried to look innocent, wounded by his allegation, her confidence more fragile now. "But sir, I told you: it was an accident."

"I see." Pausing, then pointing upwards: "Look across the street for a moment." She craned to follow his line of sight. "There: up on the top floor. Can you see?"

She gazed at the somewhat austere building, puzzled. "No, sir. I mean, the windows are dark." Passers-by were stopping in their tracks now, joining her gaze, locals perhaps fascinated by the sight of two Brits in such evident and public disagreement.

"Exactly. Government offices. We let the bureaucrats enjoy the sights of the street below, but keep the public's gaze out. That's where I've been for the past hour. A meeting with my deputy."

A frown crossed her face. "Deputy, sir? I mean, isn't that the Prime Minister's office? Do you work there, or something?"

"No, I don't. It would seem you don't recognise me." He smiled. "That's no bad thing, I suppose. Anonymity can sometimes be a blessing."

"Should I, sir? I mean, sorry and all that, but..." She racked her brains, without success.

"Allow me to introduce myself, then. Sir Marcus Willington." He paused before continuing, watching shocked recognition dawn on her face. "Her Majesty's Governor here in the protectorate of Transasia."

He stretched out his hand. She gulped, extending hers, finding it gripped tightly and shaken firmly. "Victoria Harding, sir. Pleased to meet you."

"Yes, well. Not the way in which members of the expatriate community usually choose to introduce themselves to me. Running into me like that. There's usually just a little more respect."

Too right, there was a little more respect. A whole lot more respect. She'd heard her father talk about the Governor: his reputation certainly preceded him. Victoria looked downcast. "No, sir. Sorry. I'll look where I'm going next time."

"Oh, I shall make sure of that, don't you worry. I'd been observing you for a while, you see."

"Sir?" Her mind clicked fast: what exactly had he seen?

"And what might I have noticed in the past - say, half hour, Miss Victoria? Had I happened to glance out of the window across the street?"

She paused. "Err..."

"Let me tell you what I saw, then, shall I? I saw a group of very smartly-dressed British schoolgirls careering around making idiots of themselves, bumping quite deliberately into passers by and causing annoyance and embarrassment as a result."

Victoria's friends looked as worried as she, now.

He continued. "A group of Miss McPherson's girls, as I say. But it was you who happened to bump into me. So I shall ask you for an explanation."

She thought fast. "It was just a bit of harmless fun, sir."

"Harmless fun? Harmless? For the gentleman whose coffee you spilled down his shirt? For the old lady whose shopping you left strewn across the street? Or for the mother whose young son nearly stepped in front of a tram trying to dodge you?"

"Sir, please. That wasn't me."

His voice was still measured, but he sounded annoyed: "Ah. I see. Wasn't you. So you'd like to get some of your friends into trouble, too, then?"

"No, sir, but I mean..."

"Right. I don't have all day to waste standing in the street arguing with a... sixteen-year-old?"

"Seventeen, sir." Managing to sound indignant, even in this precarious situation.

Sir Marcus turned to his two accomplices. "This is precisely the sort of thing I was discussing with the Prime Minister. Heaven knows, we have a poor enough relationship with some of the locals without our children insulting them like this." They both nodded. "And if word got out that we tolerated this sort of thing," he spluttered, gesturing to the small crowd that had gathered to observe the free entertainment, "it could undermine all of our recent efforts."

"Sir, please, it won't happen again."

As if he hadn't heard her, the Governor continued, questioning the taller of his two members of staff: "I would imagine that this could quite safely be considered under Section Five of the island's penal code?"

"Yes, sir, if you wanted to press charges."

Press charges? PRESS CHARGES? What on earth...?

"To make an example of her, I think. Show that we won't tolerate this sort of disrespectful behaviour in the midst of the expat community. Demonstrate the high esteem in which we expect our chaps to hold the locals."

The schoolgirl looked terrified. "But sir, please, really, I'm sorry, it won't..."

The Governor continued to talk to his inspector, ignoring the objections from the subject of the discussion. "Take her across to the central police station, would you."

"Yes, sir."

"No, sir, please..." (Police station? He couldn't be serious!)

"Call her father."

"Yes, sir."

"*Please*, sir..." (No, don't tell him. He'd murder me.)

"Brief the duty Punishment Officer as to the reason you've taken her in."

"Yes, sir."

(*Punishment Officer*?)

"And..." Sir Marcus delayed, as if watching for her reaction. "And have her soundly flogged."

"Yes, sir. Of course, sir. As you wish."

The policeman came towards Victoria, but she reached out to clutch the governor's hand, in panic. "No, sir, please. You can't. It's not fair..." Her girlfriends joined in the chorus of objections.

He raised a hand to silence them. "If you'd like me to have you all thrashed, I'll certainly arrange it. Never mind the police station, a short note to your fathers would presumably suffice." Some of the girls blushed, acknowledging the severity of parental methods in the colony. "But I rather suggest you keep quiet. I intend to make an example of Miss Harding, and to demonstrate to the good people of Transasia that we won't stand for this sort of conduct. Now, ladies, I must..."

The second police officer had approached the Governor, and whispered something quietly in his ear. Sir Marcus turned to him: "You know, you're right. I hadn't thought of that." He looked back at the now-pale Victoria, who was being hugged by her friends, huddled around her in a protective cordon, offering well-intentioned but quite meaningless reassurances.

"The Chief Constable here is of the opinion that it might cause some unrest with the other offenders were a British girl to be whipped. Make them a little over-excited and boisterous. I bow to his superior judgement. Chief Constable, kindly arrange for her to be taken to the Governor's Residence instead, will you? I have another meeting," glancing at his watch, "for which

I am quite embarrassingly late, and I shall administer the punishment myself when I return to my office." And with that, Sir Marcus - with scarcely a look at the petrified girl he had just sentenced - pushed through the gaggle of girls, and headed purposefully down the road.

--

Did everyone know? They certainly all seemed to look at her inquisitively - with a certain morbid fascination, perhaps.

There was the Governor's secretary opposite, a formidable lady, who must surely have been in on her fate. Hair in a tight bun, clothes frumpy enough for the Home Counties - why did so many English ladies ignore the bright linens and vivid silks of the markets on every other street corner? A veritable ogre, who'd snarled at her to hand over her identity card, and returned it shortly afterwards having studiously copied down the relevant details. No sympathy there, as Victoria sat upright in the straight-backed chair in the corridor, awaiting Sir Marcus's return and avoiding the dragon's unkind gaze.

Or the innumerable officials, who passed back and forth, adding papers to the Governor's file here, removing manila envelopes there.

What about the local maid, who'd so politely brought her a cup of tea? Sipping orange pekoe from a fine china cup: how dainty, how British. Afternoon tea at the Governor's House. How bizarre, in the circumstances. The young woman had to pinch herself to remind herself that this was real – then try to undo the pinch when she remembered that it was.

Surely not? Whipping? Flogging? Her? No. Really. An idle threat. He had been joking, though? Hadn't he? He must have been. He couldn't... She couldn't bear it if he... did. So humiliating. No: it couldn't be. Just a warning. And what about Father? Miss McPherson? The Governor was trying to scare her. Making her wait like this. Her sister: what would Katy think? When would he be back? No, he wouldn't. Couldn't. It couldn't be legal, could it? He is in charge, though. The other girls: what would they say? Had they told their parents? Presumably.

Never mind the thought that kept trying to sneak into her mind: how much could it hurt, and would she be able to cope?

Twenty minutes passed.

Forty.

An hour, ticking by noisily on the carriage clock perched on the secretary's desk.

Five-o-five. Five-fifteen, sixteen, seventeen.

Eighteen.

A commotion. The Governor, rushing past, a blur of expensive suit, important papers and pompous bureaucrats. She stood up, but he breezed past her without a glance.

Five thirty.

Five forty.

Please get it over and done with. Was the very wait to be her punishment? (Please let the wait be her punishment). (Please don't let them hurt me). (Daddy...?)

And then the officials were leaving in a flurry; a phone rang on the secretary's desk, and the guard on the door was waving her towards the Governor's office, handing her a folder to pass to Sir Marcus. And suddenly she was there in front of him, as he waved to her to close the door, taking in the opulent surroundings, watching the gentleman remove his jacket and observing that he didn't look one iota less than deadly serious. Immaculate, crisp. How could he look so cool and collected in the afternoon heat?

The room seeped privilege from every corner; reeked of years of colonial misrule.

"So, Miss Harding, I hope my staff has been hospitable?"

"Yes, sir."

"Good. Well, what do you have to say for yourself before we deal with this afternoon's little incident?"

The plea for mitigation, the speech rehearsed and re-rehearsed in the chair outside his door, sounded faint and feeble as it stumbled out: "I really promise, sir. I know we shouldn't have..."

"When I punish you, Miss Harding," (when? WHEN? Not if? Not "I've decided not to"? Please...?) "I shall be both disciplining you for your actions, and also sending out a clear message to the wider community. This is precisely the sort of behaviour that discredits the British in the eyes of the Transasians, and I'm afraid I can't have them thinking that I tolerate it."

"No, sir. But can't you just this once..."

"No I can't. If my predecessor hadn't had quite so many "just this once's", the colony wouldn't be in quite the fractious state that we're dealing with today. Now, I've spoken to Miss McPherson, and she fully supports what I'm about to do. She tells me to her surprise that you're one of her star pupils, which makes this whole episode rather depressing, I must say."

"Yes, sir." Star pupil equals good girl. One-off mistake. Second chances. PLEASE...?

"You've received corporal punishment at school?"

"No, sir."

"I suppose that if you had, you might not be here now. Seen other girls get the stick?"

"Yes, sir." Just last week, to recall just the most recent exhibition: Samantha Teasdale and Angela O'Malley. Brought out in front of assembly for cheating in a public examination. Skirts and knickers removed, bent over facing one another, touching toes - heads brushing against one another. Miss McPherson prowling from one to the other, caning them alternately. Bold, confident young women reduced to howling, obedient children, like so many before them. Victoria wished she'd not remembered.

"And the Chief Constable will tell you if you're in any doubt that I have full legal authority to take over the administration of the punishment, as the de facto head of Transasia's judicial system."

He was the Governor, after all. Her Majesty's voice. His word is our command, and all that. No lawyer, she hadn't even considered the issue. What was he going to do? Where? Here? Now? "Yes, sir."

"And I've spoken to your father, who's downstairs in the Drawing Room to take you home after we've finished."

Please no, you've not told him. Please, daddy, come up here, past the dragon on the door and save me... Please, daddy, go away and don't find out... Too late for that, though. She could picture him, waiting. Angry at her? Worried? Both? She remembered when Katy had been caned at school the previous year; her younger sister swore that her form-master's blows were nothing compared to their father's heavily-applied leather belt, laid on in her bedroom that night - thin walls doing nothing to mask the lecture, the ensuing whacks, the screams, the sobs.

Sir Marcus picked up the antique phone on his desk, "Simon, yes, hello. Could you go and fetch the cane from the staff quarters? The one they use to punish the maids? Yes, that's right. The heavier one, please. Yes, right away. There's a good chap. Thank you."

"Right, let's sign the paperwork." He reached out to take the folder from her. A solitary piece of paper lay inside, topped with a royal crest. The Governor selected a fountain pen from his desk and signed with a flourish, passing the pen to the girl to do the same.

They waited, watching each other. Standing their ground. One of them shaking, the other perfectly still.

A knock at the door, and an immaculate young man appeared, scarcely older than Victoria - presumably the aforementioned Simon, given the cane in his hand (my goodness, that's twice as thick as Miss McPherson's!). He passed the implement to his boss. "Wait outside, would you, Simon? My aide-de-camp," he explained. "You can escort young Miss Harding away once I've punished her."

The assistant glanced sympathetically at her, before retiring, confirming his agreement.

And then it was happening. As if in slow motion, the Governor had her remove her blazer, and hand it to him. He folded it carefully over his desk, and then gestured the girl to a large, ancient leather sofa. "Lift up your skirt and bend over the arm, there's a good girl."

Not happening to me.

How much will it hurt?

Thighs cold against leather. Head down, absorbing its smell.

Backside forced upwards: raised, offering a slender yet undeniably clear target.

"I shall be giving you eight strokes."

"Please, sir..." EIGHT?

"Or more if you insist?"

"No, sir."

"Now, had the police whipped you, you would have been stripped bare and tied down. I shall spare you the indignity on both counts. But should you move out of position, I shall re-apply the stroke and additionally add one extra to the overall tally. That's how we did it when I was a prefect, and I recall that it usually works."

Prefect? *Prefect?* He'd done this before, then. Prefect, like she hoped to be next year? (Not, of course, that the girls at the convent carried canes. Not like Eton, or Harrow, or wherever her inquisitor had studied the art of beating the less senior pupils).

And then she felt his fingers brush her skin, and her white knickers being lowered, the Governor lifting her slightly from the sofa so he could take them down, clear, abandoning them around her ankles.

She waited for a final lecture: Miss McPherson always proffered final words of wisdom to her victim, and hence to the wider audience. But the blow came first - unexpected, out of the blue, sudden, striking, cutting, oh my goodness it couldn't be... She shot up, hands reaching back, tears swelling in her eyes. No, please, that's too much...

"Not a good start, I'm afraid," she heard him say calmly. "It doesn't count, and your tally is up to nine. Get back in position."

"Sorry, sir."

Don't let me humiliate myself. Be brave. Be brave. Be... "Owwwwwwwwww!". Back up again, involuntarily, holding, rubbing.

Crying.

"Up to ten. I can call Simon in to restrain you, if you'd prefer?"

"Oh god no, sir, please, no."

And a pause to collect herself, and he walked away, and turned around, then arced the cane down for the third time, or her third first time, and this time she clenched her fists and gave a shriek and held on, tight, for dear life.

He patted her on the back. "Good girl. Well done. One."

One of eight. No, she'd earned an extra for each one of the first two. One now of ten.

Was the next stroke gentler? Was she just getting used to it? She clenched her teeth, concentrating, waited, still waited, prayed him to get on with it... then absorbed two more fierce cuts: searing, agonising. Be calm, don't give in, let's get it over with...Up to four... should she count the real total to herself, towards her eight? The actual strokes towards the ever-increasing sentence? Forget it and try to block out the painful sums?

Again. That one HURT. That one REALLY hurt. Tears were dripping down her cheeks now. Please, no, that was too much. Please. "If you could try to keep down the noise, there are staff working in the surrounding rooms."

"Owwww!" The sixth and the best. The worst. Was that directly on top of the previous one? Please let this stop. That's enough. I won't do it again. Promise. Honestly. On my word. Really...

Four to go. No, three. Was it? How many had she had? He'd said eight in total. Then two more for standing up. Ten in total. She'd had six, hadn't she? Four more?

Again the rod whistling through the air. A loud sob. A brave, but broken girl standing up, dancing.

"Might I suggest that you try a little harder, as you're hardly making it easy for yourself?" Nightmare unending.

The tip of the next blow landing cruelly on her left buttock. Victoria breathed deeply, fighting the instinct to reach back, to protect herself. He'd mentioned being a prefect: he had certainly not lost his skill, although she suspected his daughter may have been a more recent target than his fags.

A firm hand on her back once more. "I'll do them quickly and let's get it over with, shall we?"

A muffled "please"...

He took her hands, and made her hold the edge of the cushion. "Try not to think about them."

So she tried, and he whipped her: once, twice, up to the four she was owed, so quickly that she almost lost count, so hard that the previous strokes felt like mere tickles. And her backside was burning, swelling, and her face was sodden, and from the distance she could hear a voice telling her to stand, to dress, that she was a brave girl, that she'd done well.

And after she'd struggled with her clothes, and wiped away as many tears as she could (only for more to fall into their place), she found herself enveloped in a hug. A hug? After what he'd just done to her? But the most welcome hug ever. Reassurance, that she'd behaved exactly as a good British girl should; taken her punishment well; that she was a good girl, he knew; that she wouldn't be in trouble again; that he wished her well.

That, as he let go, he went over to the phone, and summoned his aide. "Miss Harding's whipping is over, Simon, if you'd care to escort her downstairs to the drawing room." Downstairs. Daddy.

Simon appearing beside her, as if from nowhere, taking her arm gently. And before she knew it, she was being led from the room, hearing the Governor tell Simon to hurry along so as not to keep her father waiting.

The punishment dorm

"I am absolutely exasperated at your behaviour, young lady."

"Yes, sir." Ellie stared at the ground, clasping and unclasping her hands, avoiding his gaze as she dreaded what was to follow.

Her housemaster opened the heavy leather tome on his desk, scanning the neatly-handwritten entries. "Here we are. Tuesday the seventh. Less than three weeks ago. Arguing with Mrs Johnson. Three strokes." He looked up: "I usually find that a caning is sufficient to impress the necessary lesson on a girl. Particularly when I had previously let her escape with a detention for a similar offence with the same teacher, in a misplaced moment of generosity, on the grounds of her prior excellent behaviour."

Pleading: "But I did learn from it, sir. Really..."

"Really?"

"Yes, sir." Really, she had. She thought back, the memories so fresh in her mind, un-erasable. The humiliation; the pain. The shame of becoming one of those girls whose name was recorded for posterity in the punishment ledger. The astonished, inquisitive looks on her fellow students' faces as she rejoined the class from which she had been plucked to be disciplined.

Not again...

He spoke softly, leaning forward across the desk towards her. "If you'd really learnt your lesson, Ellie, you wouldn't be here now. More to the point, you wouldn't have stormed out of Mrs Johnson's class forty minutes ago, using language that is frankly not acceptable in this - or indeed any other - school."

"But she's totally unfair. It was a good essay, and she just doesn't like me. She's stupid. I'm just not…"

His silence silenced her. They looked at each other, each waiting for the other to speak. The girl looked down: "Sorry, sir."

"I think that proves my point. You're a bright pupil, Ellie; one of our best. And almost all of your grades are excellent. But Mrs Johnson clearly believes that your work in French Literature fails to live up to the high standards that she requires. And I trust her judgement absolutely."

A pause. "Yes, sir."

"More to the point, I am not prepared for one of the girls in my house to continue to insult one of my colleagues. And I am certainly not going to accept that any girl has the right to flounce out of a classroom in temper."

Quietly, now: "No, sir."

"I certainly hope that you understand, Ellie. This time. And I intend to make sure that you do." He stood up: the trembling girl scarcely needed to watch him, the recording of that earlier afternoon replaying in her mind. The walk over to the back corner of the room; the sound of jangling keys from behind her; the creaking cupboard door, opening then closing. The cane cupboard. His walk back to the front of the room.

Puzzling. Instead of the rod that she had expected - dreaded, the housemaster held a piece of paper in his hands. He sat down again, and took out his fountain pen.

"I am not going to cane you again, Ellie. If two lectures from me, a detention and a sound dose of corporal punishment don't get through to you, I have no confidence that administering a further caning to you now will guarantee your future good behaviour." He scribbled on the form, and folded it into an envelope, which he carefully sealed and addressed.

Her housemaster looked up, handing her the packet. "You are to take this letter immediately to the deputy headmaster, in his study. It's my request to him to admit you to the Punishment Dormitory for a period of 72 hours, or until he is convinced that you have learnt the error of your ways."

"No, sir." She felt the tears welling up; what she'd done wasn't bad enough to merit the Punishment Dorm, surely?

"I'm not going to discuss it with you, girl. That is my decision, and I am convinced that it is in your best interests. Now, hurry along." He screwed the lid back onto his fountain pen, and waved her to the door.

--

Dr. Jenkins, St. Clair's deputy headmaster, is a man both loved and feared. Loved, as a brilliant scholar and inspiring teacher; good-humoured, kind; a shoulder on which the girls could, and often did cry when they needed someone trustworthy to whom they could turn in the absolute confidence that he always maintained. Yet feared, too.

In many ways, punishment at the hands of the deputy headmaster could be viewed as the school's ultimate deterrent. Certainly, some girls found that their disciplinary path led into the office of the headmaster himself, but by the time they found themselves in that unwelcome situation, it was most often to hear confirmation of their expulsion from the establishment; any thrashings that he administered were therefore more final retribution than corrective punishment.

Dr. Jenkins, on the other hand, focused on bringing around rapid improvements in the behaviour of those girls whose housemasters had found the usual disciplinary methods to be ineffective. Girls like Ellie.

He'd been pleased to see her, at first. Surprised, perhaps, that one of his star pupils would have knocked on his door when she should presumably have been in class, but welcoming nonetheless. Offered her a seat on his sofa; asked how the rehearsals were progressing for the school musical ("I have to admit that Oklahoma is far from my favourite work, but I am confident that you will bring out the best in it.").

He sat opposite her, sinking into a deep leather armchair. Reassuring, sympathetic: "You do look a little upset, my dear, if I may say so. Is anything the matter?"

She nodded, the tears that she'd vowed to keep back welling up once more. She reached into her blazer pocket, and pulled out the envelope, which she held out to him, her fingers trembling.

Jenkins walked over to his desk, taking a letter knife and carefully opening the envelope. He read carefully, then turned round to look at the distraught girl.

"Really, Ellie?"

"Yes, sir. I'm sorry, sir. Really. I mean..."

"The time for explaining yourself is well past; it was for your housemaster to assess your attitude to your offence, and your degree of repentance. My role now is purely to ensure that the punishment that he has requested is administered, in a way that will prevent your future misbehaviour. Even if I am surprised to see you, of all girls, sitting before me in this predicament."

"Sorry, sir..."

"Well, Miss Mitchell, I'm sure you've heard rumours about how the Punishment Dormitory operates."

She nodded, noticing the immediate change from her first name to the more formal address. Rumours? Of course. The Punishment Dorm was the stuff of girls' nightmares from the moment they entered the College. Nightmares that she was going to have to live for real. Yet, like a nightmare, it still felt implausible: was this really happening? To her?

Jenkins glanced at his watch: "You have seventeen minutes before the final lesson of the day begins. I want you to go back to your own dormitory, quickly, and pick up all of your uniform, including any sports kit that you may need. Nothing else. Take it to Matron, and ask her to show you to the Punishment Dorm; leave your things by the bed that she will allocate to you, and tidy everything away into a wardrobe when you return there after the final lesson is over.

"She will also hand you a document to read; you should study it very carefully, as I shall check that you understand it fully when I see you in the office that I have next to the dorm at 5.30 this evening. Understood?"

Ellie nodded.

He passed her a booklet from his desk: "And you'll need to present this to your teachers at the end of each lesson; they'll know what to do with it. Now, girl: fifteen minutes, and make sure you're not late."

--

The next quarter-of-an-hour went in a flash; a rush back to her dorm; throwing her clothes into a bag; a dash to Matron's office; being shown upstairs in the East Wing (so *that's* where it was) to the Punishment Dorm - six neatly-made beds, a high-backed wooden chair next to each; three wardrobes, bare walls. Her bed the one in the far corner; bag thrown underneath, the oh-so-important document that Matron had given her placed on the bed to read later; a hasty journey back to room 17, the venue for the final lesson of the day. English Lit, thank goodness - she couldn't have faced Mrs Johnson.

She almost made it on time - two, perhaps three minutes late. The class was already working, silently by the time she arrived, and Mr Robertson raised a quizzical eyebrow at her late arrival. Ears pricked up around the classroom at the news that Ellie had been with the deputy head - news of her argument with Mrs J had clearly done the rounds. Ellie sent to Jenkins - did that mean....?

She didn't have her books with her, of course - she'd forgotten to stop at her locker on the way to the classroom. Robertson joked weakly that she must have known the text by heart: would she care to recite it to the class? And all the time, all she wanted to do was run and hide; to escape; actually, most of all, to know what was on that document that Matron had handed to her, headed 'Punishment Dormitory Rules'. Ellie glanced across the room at Carolyn Bennett - a previous Dorm resident: what would she find if she could sneak inside Carolyn's mind, download her memory?

The other girls wanted to talk after the final bell - to quiz her or to tease, she didn't know. But she remembered Jenkins' instructions - time to tidy her things away, and read that document. Ignoring her friends, she fled back to the Dorm, hoping noone observed where she was heading.

Two other girls were already in the dorm when she returned - she recognised them both: Livia Richards and Tilly Morgan-Young, both from the Lower Sixth. Ellie tried to sound cheerful: "Hi. I see we're all in this together." But neither girl answered; Livia raised her finger to her lips: "Shhhhhhhhhh".

Tidying her things away came first: she found an empty wardrobe, and threw in her uniform, kicking her bag back out of sight. And then she perched on the edge of the bed, and started reading…

--

ST. CLAIR'S COLLEGE
PUNISHMENT DORMITORY RULES

1. Girls must attend all school commitments as usual (assemblies, chapel, lessons, prep classes, sports, scheduled rehearsals for official school plays, music practice and other formal College activities). Meals will be taken as usual, but girls must sit at the designated Punishment Dormitory table at the rear of the dining room. When not required for such activities, girls must return to the Punishment Dormitory immediately.

2. The Dormitory must be kept immaculately neat, clean and tidy at all times. Other than when cleaning or tidying, girls will spend their time in the Dorm sitting neatly on the chair adjacent to their bed, during which time they may read a textbook directly related to their current studies. The Dormitory door must be left open at all times.

(Ellie bolted onto the chair as quickly as she could).

3. There must be no talking in the Dormitory at any time.

(No wonder they'd hushed her).

4. Evening inspection will be at 8.30pm. At this time, girls will be standing beside their bed, wearing their dressing gowns. Lights out will be immediately following evening inspection.

(8.30? They can't send us to bed at 8.30?!)

5. Reveille will be at 6.30am. Girls will shower, and then queue in silence in their dressing gowns outside the deputy headmaster's office (adjacent to the Punishment Dormitory). The deputy headmaster will then review each girl's performance over the previous 24 hours, based on the written reports which must be completed at the end of every lesson and other school activity, and left under his office door before 8pm the previous evening.

(Damn, damn, damn. She'd forgotten to give it to Robertson to fill in. Damn… Oh no…)

6. During this morning meeting, each girl will receive her allotted daily punishment.

(Allotted punishment? What on earth was that? She could guess…)

7. For the duration of their period as residents of the Punishment Dormitory, girls are expected to demonstrate the highest standards of behaviour at all times. All standard College Rules continue to apply; where these rules contradict the usual College Rules, these rules will take precedence.

8. At the end of her allocated time in the Punishment Dormitory, each girl will be interviewed by the deputy headmaster and their housemaster, who will together determine whether the offender may re-join the usual school routine, or whether further time should be spent in the Dormitory.

(Damn. Like, it might be more than 72 hours?)

9. Girls may not communicate any information regarding the Punishment Dormitory to other pupils, or speak to other pupils at any time unless required to do so by a member of staff.

10. Failure to comply with these Rules will result in punishment, at the sole discretion of the deputy headmaster.

--

Ellie breathed in, deeply. Although the rules didn't mention the specifics of the punishments that were to be applied, she feared the worst: and that mention of 'allotted punishments' was scary. If only she could ask the others - but they stared intently at their textbooks as if they were the most fascinating books on earth, maintaining a monk-like silence.

She glanced at her watch: five o'clock. Thirty minutes until her appointment with Jenkins. She set to work, learning the rules…

--

"Hold out your hands, palms upwards, with your right hand on top of your left." Her arms shook with nerves, as she tried to hold her hands still - and to avoid giving away her fear.

He drew the thick strap back, and cracked it down. Numbing at first. And then the pain… Oh, the pain, as if a hot coal had been pressed momentarily into her palm and then withdrawn.

"Swap hands…"

WHACK! Oh, God it hurt….

She'd tried to learn the rules. Really, she had.

"Swap."

A moment's pause, before the next burning blow.

She swapped, without prompting.

She had known what they said. Really. Just some of the detail: "What's Rule Five?" She couldn't remember the order in which they were listed. And reveille - 6.30? She'd though 7 o'clock.

THWACK!

The last of the four blows. Two for each mistake.

"You may leave. Shut the door behind you."

That was it. Nothing more. No discussion, no time for apology. She skulked back to the Dorm, hands cradled in her armpits. Go away, tears: mustn't show the other girls that I'm weak.

They'd heard, of course. Jenkins' office was next door - sound must have carried through the thin walls, her punishment overheard. Had they listened sympathetically, or blocked out the sounds?

Livia smiled faintly at her, reassuringly. Tilly stared down at her book.

Ellie returned to her chair. She hadn't known to bring a textbook, of course. Placing her reddened palms upwards, blowing down on them from the corner of her mouth, she looked up at the clock: dinner was approaching.

--

Their table at the rear of the dining room was a lonely place. Exposed to the gaze of the other students - some mocking, some sympathetic. The same food, the same *horrible* food as always. But eaten as if in a goldfish bowl - watched, observed, discussed. "Ellie Mitchell's in the Punishment Dorm!" "Little Miss Goody-Goody's in trouble." "I wonder what really happens?" "I hope she's OK." And was that a flicker of a smile on Mrs Johnson's face?

Prep followed: ninety minutes to complete that day's homework. Less than Ellie usually spent - she frequently beavered away until late, snug in a corner of the library. Only 72 hours, though: she'd be able to catch up. At least, she hoped it would only be 72 hours... Classmates wanted to talk, but knew she couldn't - this was like being sent to Coventry in reverse. Terrible. Horrible. Humiliating.

--

Back in the dorm, the other girls glanced at each other at 8.20, and started to undress, folding their clothes and placing them in their wardrobes. Ellie took the hint, and copied. Indeed, she'd only just clambered into pyjamas and dressing gown and made it to the side of her bed, when Jenkins walked in.

Carrying a slipper, she noticed. Well, more of a gym shoe, pump. So this inspection carried consequences, did it? Of course, she should have realised. Please let me pass...

He went to Tilly first: lifted her chin with his finger, inspected her face. For what? Make-up, she guessed. Jenkins checked her bed; opened and closed her wardrobe. Picked up the book from her bedside chair: "'Advanced Level Calculus' - a good read, Miss Morgan-Young?" "It's very well-explained, sir." "Good. Well, young lady, you have passed the inspection. Bed."

Obligingly, Tilly removed her dressing gown and hung it on the peg above her chair. She climbed, naked, beneath the sheets, and turned onto her side, her relief palpable.

Please let me pass...

Livia was next. The same routine - terrified girl faces master with eye for detail. An eye that picked up the stain on her school tie, hanging in the wardrobe. That noticed that her bed was made up incorrectly. Who picked out the dust on the top of her chair's back.

Who made her remove her dressing gown, hang it up, then bend over the end of her bed.

Ellie seeing all from her position on the opposite side of the dorm. Noticing Livia's already-marked backside. Tilly still on her side, deliberately looking away.

Both hearing the whack, whack, whack as the plimsoll descended three times, once for each mistake. Both hearing the, "Not good enough, Miss Richards," as the girl was sent to her bed.

Please let me pass...

Please let me pass...

"Settling in, Miss Mitchell?"

"Yes, sir."

"I thought we had discussed the Dormitory Rules earlier, Miss Mitchell?"

"Yes, sir," she blushed.

"Recite Rule Four to me, please."

"Sir, that Evening inspection will be at 8.30, and that we should be standing next to our beds by then in our dressing gowns."

He waited.

"Sir....?"

"When you re-read Rule Four in the morning, Miss Mitchell, you will note that it adds that 'Lights out will be immediately following evening inspection'. It also states that girls will be 'wearing their dressing gowns'. Not 'wearing their pyjamas and dressing gowns'. Remove the offending items this minute; place your pyjamas in your wardrobe, hang up your dressing gown, and stand by your bed with your hands behind your back."

Never could she have conceived of a situation in which she would be hurrying to strip in front of the school's deputy head, but Ellie was back by her bed, naked within thirty seconds. Bare, exposed. Humiliated, and not for the first time today.

His inspection was thorough. "This bed is creased." (From where she'd sat on it when she arrived, presumably). "There's a bag under the bed: all belongings should be in your wardrobe. And there's enough dust under here to make me sneeze for weeks."

And then he opened the wardrobe. Ellie bit her lip: she knew now that the 'fling the clothes in' approach would fall far short of his exacting standards. Knew it. Before he turned to her: "I have never seen such a mess. By this time tomorrow, girl, your clothes will be hung up neatly, or immaculately folded. In the meantime, bend over your bed."

Being punished was bad enough. Being punished with two other girls in the room was worse. Far worse.

The slipper hurt, oh so badly. Quick blows, delivered without mercy: she lost count after the fourth, as the tears started to flow. And they flowed because she was here, in the Punishment Dorm. They flowed because she was being punished, bare; being punished by this man she respected so much. They flowed because it HURT. They flowed most of all because she knew she'd failed to achieve the standards that girls in the Dorm had to meet.

The spanking ceased, and Jenkins spoke to her clearly: "Stay in position for two minutes, then get into bed." She heard him walk away, and flick the light switch, plunging the room into darkness. And then, when he was gone, and enough time had passed, she felt her way around the bed and clambered in, the sheets cold against her throbbing behind, easing yet pressing.

Her sobs, muffled into the pillow, broke the silence. Her sobs, after a while, rocked her to sleep, to strange dreams of dark forests, deserted houses and evil men.

--

"WAKE UP, INTO THE SHOWERS". The light snapped on, as Matron burst in on them at 6.30 sharp.

Ellie swung out of bed, shocked, still half-asleep, her feet landing on the cold tiled floor. Blinking rapidly, she looked at the other girls for an example, and grabbed her dressing gown before following them out of the dormitory and along the corridor.

"You first," Matron instructed Livia, pushing her through the open door. She emerged again barely three minutes later, shivering: Matron pointed down the corridor: "You, wait outside the deputy headmaster's office. And you," she grabbed Ellie, "in the shower and be quick about it."

Ellie struggled for a moment with the controls: she couldn't work out how to get the hot water to flow. And then she realised, picturing Livia shivering before her, that there was no hot water. She climbed into the freezing stream, and washed as quickly as she could, before drying herself on the already-wet towel used by the previous girl.

Second in the queue for her appointment with Jenkins. The review of the previous day. Tilly joined them: three girls shivering, from cold and from fear.

But no sign of Jenkins…. They waited.

And waited. Still no sign.

And still no sign.

And then here he was, gown fluttering as he came through the door at the end of the corridor, and beckoned Livia to follow him.

He did not close the door.

They heard brief murmurs of conversation - Jenkins' soft voice barely audible, Livia's 'Yes, sir's and 'No, sir's occasionally reaching their ears. And then a sound that made them both wince: a sound so familiar to Ellie from three weeks before; the sound of a stick cutting through the air and landing against its soft target. Four times, each mixing Ellie's sympathy for the younger girl with her own rising panic.

Livia emerged, and gestured to Ellie to go in. It was a small room; Jenkins stood next to the desk on the left-hand side, cane in hand. A wooden chair faced the wall ahead of her. "Bend over the back of the chair, Miss Mitchell, and lift up your dressing gown."

She stepped forward, obeying his instructions. It hadn't been like this with her housemaster: her punishment then had been preceded by a lengthy discussion and lecture.

"Reach right forward. Thank you." Her backside felt taut, exposed.

"Your housemaster recommended that your daily punishment for the offences for which you were sent here should be three strokes. I shall add another two for your failure to provide me with your written report yesterday." (Oh no... how could she have forgotten?) "Did you have it completed during the last lesson of the day?"

"No, sir."

"Then another stroke for that, too. And ask the member of staff concerned to complete it retrospectively at some point today."

"Yes, sir."

And then she felt the cold wood being measured across her buttocks, and braced herself for the first stroke.

It was excruciating. Of course. She knew it would be, from last time. But somehow the memory dampens the pain, makes it seem less real.

But this was real. So real. Evenly-timed strokes, delivered with intent. Each building on the agony of the previous blows; each bringing her closer to the tears that she fought back.

Three had been bad enough at her housemaster's hands. But three of Jenkins' strokes merely took the pain of the whipping to a peak: the following three pushed the pain along a plateau, renewing and intensifying the anguish.

And then he was telling her to tidy herself up and leave.

All over. So quick. And yet two more such sessions to follow, on the next two mornings. She shuddered at the thought.

Back in the Dorm, she noticed that Livia was already in her uniform. The thrashed girls avoided one another's eyes. Ellie dressed, as carefully and neatly as she knew how - to the soundtrack of poor Tilly's howls from the neighbouring room. By the time the third of the musketeers reappeared, it was obvious that the last girl had taken the morning's longest and hardest whipping: a thought as reassuring (thank goodness I didn't get it that badly) as it was scary (but what about tomorrow...?).

--

There are days when time speeds by; every minute too short, every hour passing too quickly. At other times, the clock switches to slow-motion.

This was to be a slow-mo day.

Breakfast in the morning - her discomfort of sitting on her freshly-caned backside exacerbated by the certain knowledge that many of the girls staring at her from across the room would realise what she'd just been through.

At the end of each lesson, the crushing humiliation of having to explain to each teacher that she needed her report card updating. Their looks of surprise, tempered for some with expressions of sympathy. Comments, initials, and a tick: "Excellent, Good, Satisfactory, Poor." All 'Excellent's, so far, thank goodness: there must be some advantage to being a model pupil for most of the time.

Dodging questions and comments from her fellow students... Noting which girls offered her their sympathy and support; seeing which made the clever, snide, mortifying comments that she so hated.

Lunchtime - the same routine with dining, followed by a humiliating period queuing outside the Staff Common Room praying that Mr Robertson would emerge to sign the previous day's report entry, before scampering back to the Dormitory. Twenty minutes spare, spent sitting on the Dorm chairs, waiting for the bell that would signal the afternoon's lessons.

A double session straight after lunch with Mrs Johnson. Ellie lying low, working hard, the class seeming to drag on forever. The contented smirk on the woman's face as she signed the card: 'Good', to Ellie's relief. And then a music lesson: the chance to de-stress, with forty minutes' piano practice with cheerful old Mr Scott, who nearly fell off his piano stool when asked to sign the report, and gave her a friendly hug as she left.

She was a good girl. Really she was. It was all a mistake, her being in the Punishment Dormitory. Just a silly mistake, of which she was frequently reminded, by tasks, by comments, and by the ache in her behind.

--

That night's evening inspection was going to be different. Very different. She was going to make sure she complied; escaped. Careful clothes-folding; her bed made and re-made three times; her report card delivered on time; standing bolt upright next to her bed at 8.27. Each girl busy as a bee, albeit a silent bee - preparing themselves, protecting themselves.

Ellie's efforts even raised a 'Good' from Jenkins, who chose her for the first of his inspections. Livia, too, sailed through with flying colours.

It was as if Jenkins was saving himself for Tilly: the one girl who'd escaped punishment the previous evening, and who'd taken that morning's worst thrashing. Nothing met the deputy head's high standards: the way her bed was made, the dust on top of her wardrobe, her insufficiently-polished shoes, her un-ironed school shirt, the dirty hockey kit in the bottom of the cupboard.

Her attitude... Telling Jenkins that he was victimising her, when he asked why she had failed the inspection so dismally, was not the brightest of ideas. He stormed out of the room, reappearing moments later with the strap he'd used to punish Ellie's hands the previous afternoon. Yet it wasn't Tilly's hands that he whipped: the naked girl adopted the usual evening position, over the end of her bed, and endured (scarcely endured) a dozen or more lashes across her already-tender backside.

Yet when Jenkins had left, and Ellie whispered a soft, "Are you OK?", Tilly could only answer, "Shhhh, he might hear," and return to her sobbing.

--

Another full day. Almost routine by now.

If being last in the queue to be bent over a chair and caned could ever really be described as routine.

Thank goodness, Tilly - already crying before she went in - was dealt with first, yet again with a severity that scared Ellie senseless. Nine strokes, she counted through the open door, drawing howls and yelps of agony.

Livia went next: Ellie counted once more. Three, this morning. She'd had four yesterday, hadn't she? Ellie surmised that one of the previous day's must therefore have been for something on her report card.

When Ellie's turn arrived, it was something on her report card that caught Jenkins' eye. She'd barely checked Mr Robertson's belated entry after he'd updated the booklet after lunch - pleased that he'd given her a 'Good'. Jenkins was less impressed with her late arrival and forgotten textbook, about which the teacher had commented.

Three extra strokes. Six in total, once again. Six searing, agonising blows. Surely it should get less painful, the more one is punished, the more used to it one gets? Maybe he was caning her harder. Maybe it never gets easier...?

--

She was less of a celebrity today, she noticed. The other girls were getting used to her status; the fact that Miss Ellie Mitchell had been sent to the Punishment Dorm was no longer hot news, no longer novel. In a way, that hurt more - yeah, that Ellie, she's the sort of girl who gets into trouble, you know?

The morning progressed smoothly, until the first lesson after morning break. A French vocab test, something she'd usually have sailed through with full marks. Perhaps it was the constraints on her time - ninety minutes' study the evening before, with no extra time in her beloved library. Perhaps her mind was elsewhere. The discomfort of sitting still for lengthy periods hardly helped. But 65 per cent was scarcely up to her usual standards, and brought a dreaded 'Poor' on her report card.

Mr Robertson's English Lit class in the afternoon was no better: a 'B minus' grade on the paper she'd written two nights previously, rather than her usual 'A'; another 'Poor'. "That's not fair," she retorted: "B minus isn't poor - it's better than most of the class."

'Argued with my assessment of her disappointing performance in the class' was the comment he wrote. She knew how Jenkins would respond. "Please, Mr Robertson - can't you delete that? I wasn't arguing, just checking." To which he inserted a 'persistently' after the word 'argued' in his comments.

And then, when she returned to the Punishment Dorm at the end of the afternoon, both Tilly and Olivia were gone. She supposed she should have been relieved for them, their sentences over; the solitude merely made her anxiety greater.

If dinner was bad - sitting alone at the separate dining table - that evening's inspection was worse. Jenkins inspected every corner of the room, finding fault wherever he looked - even rubbish left by the other girls, that Ellie had overlooked. "Never mind the fact it's not in your part of the room, the Rules state that the Dormitory must be kept clean and tidy. The fact that you're the only person here doesn't invalidate the Rule."

She took six agonising whacks of the plimsoll. As she lay in bed afterwards, she reflected that a slippering should scarcely hurt, in comparison to the canings to which she was now becoming reluctantly accustomed. Yet as a method of punishment, it seemed particularly effective - re-igniting the dampened fires of the morning's thrashing, in addition to its own unsubtle pain. That, she decided, was presumably exactly why Jenkins chose to use it.

--

Her final morning. Or, at least, she hoped and prayed it was to be her final morning – whilst she dreaded what was to come.

No one to hide behind in the queue for Jenkins' office. "We'll deal with this in stages," he informed her as she adopted her position over his chair, lifting her dressing gown clear of her backside. "Your usual morning allocation, first."

Damn, damn, damn. They hurt, Jenkins swinging the cane high and laying into her with all of his strength.

Two more for the 'Poor' in French. "Girls of your calibre have high standards to meet, and it's particularly disappointing when you fail to meet them." Both excruciating; low strokes - adjacent to each other, just touching. The weals from those would be agonising to sit on during the day.

"And then we turn our attention to the fact that you still seem to view arguing with teachers as acceptable."

From her position over the back of the chair: "I didn't...."

"Point proven."

She remained silent. He continued: "I am minded to add up the strokes you had received before this morning, and re-administer them to you, since they were clearly ineffective." She shuddered, not daring to add them up. "However, I think that a further six may suffice."

A further six? Surely... OWWWWW... How was she going to survive this? Not fighting it, for one thing: she let the tears flow freely. The next three strokes landed across virtually the same path, each harder than the previous. And then he took his time for the final trio - spacing them out, ensuring that their message had reached home.

And then, just as before, the perfunctory dismissal - and she was back in the dorm, face down on her bed, sobbing as she'd never sobbed before.

--

Ellie spent the day on auto-pilot, scarcely conscious of the world around her. She picked up 'Good's on her report card; she didn't have the emotional or physical energy to 'Excel'. Her closest friends glanced across at her from time-to-time, worried about her well-being; she brushed off their queries with a none-too-convincing, "I'm fine."

She scarcely ate a morsel of her lunch. Three worries fought for concern in her mind. She had a lesson with Mrs Johnson after lunch: would she manage to stay out of trouble, or would the teacher be out to make a point? Would her 'arguing' of the previous day count against her at the end of her 72 hours, and see her stay in the Dorm extended? And what would it be like, re-emerging into normal school life, to questions, taunts and (hopefully) hugs?

Mrs Johnson was fine. Her attitude - and the 'Excellent' she recorded at the end of the class - seemed to gloat, "I've won." And, Ellie reflected, she probably had.

It was mid-afternoon when Matron appeared at the door of classroom and asked Miss Mitchell to report to the deputy headmaster's study. Twenty pairs of eyes followed her to the door.

She was taken not to Jenkins' small office next to the Punishment Dorm, but to his study in the main school building. The deputy headmaster and her housemaster were both waiting, sitting on the sofa, and stood up as she entered. They offered her a seat in the armchair. The atmosphere seemed as welcoming as could be expected, in the circumstances.

"Tell me, Ellie, what have you learnt about yourself in the past 72 hours," Jenkins enquired.

She paused. Was there a right answer to give? "I guess... that I probably don't always think before I open my mouth. That I don't like being in trouble. That I don't want to go through this again."

They both looked at her and smiled. Her housemaster spoke first: "I hear you've been a brave girl, Ellie."

"I've tried, sir."

He continued. "Dr. Jenkins and I both believe that you have learnt your lesson well. Especially after you were dealt with this morning following your discussion with Mr Robertson yesterday."

She bowed her head, ashamedly. "Yes, sir."

Jenkins stood up. "Your time in the Punishment Dormitory is completed, Ellie. Don't come back in a hurry."

She shook her head, ruefully: "I won't, sir. Thank you, sir."

"Go and pick your things up, and take them back to your usual dorm."

"Yes, sir." She turned to leave.

"And one other thing, Ellie." It was Jenkins again.

"Yes, sir?"

"It's the 'Excellent' pupils like you that make St. Clair's the great school it is. And don't you ever forget that."

"Thank you, sir." And, tears of shame mixing with tears of relief and tears of pride, she left the study and emerged a free girl once more into the long, portrait-lined corridor, ready to face the other students...

Middlington

In the early days after the Conflict, the miscreant daughters of the more prominent members of the new governing Party might have been forgiven had they believed themselves to be above the law. Not that the law was easy to define, of course, what with new regulations appearing on the statute books on an almost daily basis.

Woe betide any ordinary citizens caught committing crimes: justice in the new world was swift and severe. The Committee was very clear in its philosophy: offenders must be taught to understand the absolute authority of the State.

Yet victims of thefts, assaults, slanders, saw charges dropped without reason against certain offenders. A privileged youngster could emerge from the gated Party zones, run riot and return home with no risk of adverse consequences. Diplomatic immunity applied, for the sometimes least diplomatic young ladies. Yet no ordinary citizen would dare object: any hint of complaint led the Community Defenders to – and often straight through - one's front door.

The New Manor case changed things, inevitably. You won't need reminding of the details, I'm sure: the pictures of the baying crowds besieging the Committee's local HQ are indelibly ingrained in the collective memory. The Defenders brought in reenforcements; the mob grew in size in direct proportion to the degree of violence being used to try to quell the dispute.

Eventually, an offer was made before discontent spread to other regions. "We are a community of equals now," President Russell had proclaimed. "Justice is the right of every citizen. Every citizen shares its obligations. And no citizen can escape its retribution should they offend its principles."

So the rabble dispersed; the two girls responsible – daughters of the new elite - were tried. The floggings to which they were sentenced were administered in private, but the grainy images of the official recording crept onto the CommitteeWeb. Russell's edict to Party members made it clear: no special treatment, no exceptions, no tolerance of wayward offspring who might compromise the Committee's work.

If anything, indeed, the standards for family members of those in the Party became even more demanding. The 'rights of every citizen' seemed to require arrests for the most innocent misdemeanours. Middlington was commandeered in about the third month after the start of the clampdown. "Of course we'll punish them if we have to," the President explained in private, "but there's no need to force our family members to mix with inappropriate types whilst we do so."

There were sixty or so girls in residence at any time – although the official numbers showed more, the public being reassured by the severity of the Party's clampdown on 'its own'. The sandstone turrets hid behind a high wall, deep inside a thick forest: easy for the authorities to protect from prying eyes, and straightforward to secure once its original owners had been 'invited' to relocate.

Not even in her darkest nightmares would Amy have ever pictured herself within its walls. She knew of Middlington's existence: who didn't? But it was for bad, bad girls: her spat with the StateBucks manager was hardly the stuff of the courts, of criminals. She might have sworn once, but his attitude when she'd complained was enough to upset anyone. Her coffee had been knocked over accidentally, not thrown over him as he'd alleged. The Community Defenders had barged into her as they rushed into the shop: she certainly hadn't assaulted them, as the witnesses seemed to suggest.

But these were interesting times. A quick glance at her identity papers had confirmed her status. The Official Arbiter was called from the barracks; the good citizens hastily rounded up from the market square to form a jury were scarcely likely to be favourably-disposed to the daughter of such a senior Committee official. It could have been no more than two hours from spilt coffee to "Guilty as charged", and the cold metal handcuffs being clamped around her delicate wrists as they were forced behind her back.

The Arbiter looked at her, observing her plight. He spoke softly. "It's your first offence, I see."

"Yes, sir." Don't argue, she thought: be polite.

"That's a shame. Always a pity, when a girl from such a good background dishonours her family – and thus lets the Committee down too."

"Sir, I didn't intend to…"

He raised a hand to silence her. "We've been through what happened." He took out a pen, and wrote slowly, carefully on a sheet of paper, passing it to a court officer. "Thirty days in Middlington. Fifty strokes of the birch. Take her away…"

"Nooooooooooo…!"

The Arbiter, already leaving the courtroom, turned: "You would be well-advised to remain silent, young lady, lest I feel compelled to change my mind and impose a less lenient sentence. Take her away!"

--

The van was cold, dirty. She sat in the darkness, wedged into the corner, her tears melting the dried mud on the metal floor. She'd tried to stand, but the cuffs made balancing impossible.

They stopped after an hour: she could just about see her watch if she wriggled her arms. Were they there already? She clambered unsteadily to her feet, bracing herself for the unknown. And then the van jerked into life, tumbling her to the floor.

It stopped again, not much further on. This time…. "Try to stay composed, Amy," she murmured to herself. "No matter what…" But again, the engine roared.

Three times more they stopped. Game-playing. Unsettling her. Making her prepare, to ready herself each time for the moment of arrival; then dragging out the journey some more. By the time the van started bumping up a steep hill, she was almost willing them to arrive at their destination; as the doors were flung open, she would have given anything for another few miles in the truck.

It was dark; the air outside was cold. The hands that pulled her to the ground firm but not unkind. His accent struck her immediately: the distinctive burr of the Northern Segment, that she'd scarcely heard since the Committee introduced its zoning regulations some three years before.

"This way." He unlocked a heavy door, and led her inside. It shut, firm, behind her. "Welcome to Middlington." Polite. Not unpleasant, from the man who was about to deprive her of her freedom.

More doors, more locks. Keys, combinations: impossible to memorise. The guard must have read her mind: "One girl did try and escape, in the early days. Got through two doors somehow. Then got stuck. We left her for a few hours before going to retrieve her."

"What happened to her?"

"She was dealt with the following morning. In front of the other girls." He shook his head at the memory. "They laid it on hard, poor lass. Now, we need to sort out some papers, then everything will be in order."

Why weren't they shouting at her? Why was he so damned nice? He uncuffed her wrists, now sore and marked. He asked her if she would remove her clothes. Asked, as if enquiring whether she would like a cup of tea. She glanced around for the changing room, a curtain maybe; there was none. As she undressed, hesitantly, the officer went to a cupboard in the corner, pulling out a blue T-shirt and grey, elasticated trousers. He waited until she was bare, bade her fold her own garments neatly, and exchanged the Middlington prison uniform for her neat pile of designer labels. Jewellry too –earings, locket, watch: all were passed over to his custody.

"It's after lights out. You'll be in Group 5. They're not bad girls." And he commanded her to follow him through the dimly-lit corridors, eventually pausing outside a brightly-painted door. He unlocked it, and barked an announcement: "Officer present!"

Girls staggered sleepily from under the sheets, emerging naked, wobbling to their feet. The officer pointed to the furthest bed, next to which stood a small, pale, fair-haired girl.

"You can share with Becky. Clothes folded neatly on the chair next to your side of the bed. Silence in the dormitory. The others will show you what to do in the morning." And he shut the door behind him.

He'd left the light on, she noticed. They always did, she later discovered. It made the CCTV images in the control room so much clearer.

She must have looked as disorientated as she felt. The other girls were clambering back into their beds – no words of welcome, merely resentful looks for their disturbed sleep. Her bedmate beckoned to her; she walked across, removed the uniform, and slipped into the bed, shivering.

"I'm Amy," she whispered.

"Becky," quietly, right into her ear, "but they don't allow us to talk." Becky. Who held her tight, despite the rules, under their shared starched white sheet, as Middlington's newest inmate cried herself to a restless sleep.

--

Someone had certainly invested considerable attention to detail when designing the Middlington regime. When the bell woke her the next morning, Amy had glanced around for a clock. It was early, for sure: still dark outside. But no timepieces could be found. Not in the dorm, not anywhere in the building. The girls had forfeited the right to the time.

Just the bell, whenever something had to be done.

The dorms. Girls thrown in troupes of twelve, banned from communicating with their fellow residents. They dined at adjacent tables, and caught occasional fleeting glimpses of the other residents during the day: scared girls, like themselves, dressed identically but living parallel lives. Were the other groups subject to the same rules, the same treatment? They'd never know.

The silence. Always, silence. Silence on waking, silence in the early morning showers – even when the supervising officer flicked the switch to turn off the heat and pour the final thirty seconds of water onto them on the bitterest of cold settings. Silence at all times other than meals, and when spoken to by a member of staff. (Breakfast gave Amy her first chance to speak since arriving: names were exchanged, reassurances offered).

The staff. Recruited from the ranks of the Party's most trusted. Men and women who had distinguished themselves during the Conflict. Who'd served loyally. Who could be trusted to stand no nonsense. Impeccably polite; awesomely intimidating.

The daily routine. A stretch copying out President Russell's speeches. Bell. A spell sitting in closely-supervised silence. Bell. The opportunity to memorise passages from The Committee's rule book. Bell. Lunch, with another chance to talk: scraps of backgrounds emerging, advice shared with the newcomer on what to do ("follow their instructions, to the letter") and what not (anything else).

Bell. A period of physical training in the gymnasium: sit-ups and running and climbing. Bell. A test on the memorised passages from The Committee's rule book. Jess's face when she misquoted rule 65.4; her outstretched hands trembled as the Officer took out his strap, and cracked it down fiercely. Twice on each hand. Bell.

An interlude cleaning their room. The inspection, girls standing to attention at the end of their beds. Martha and Samantha, whose sheet showed signs of creasing invisible to all but the most pedantic eye, lowering their trousers, bending over their metal bedsteads, taking three whacks each with the inspector's cane. Becky, trembling as the officer drew near; shaking as he knelt down, running his finger on the linoleum under the bed. Holding it up, in front of her eyes.

Clean. "Well done."

Bell. Another opportunity to enjoy His Excellency The President's collected works. Bell. Supper. Bell. A spell polishing cutlery in the kitchens. Bell. Scrubbing corridors, tidying rooms.

Bell. Stripping, folding their clothes. Bed. Silence, broken only by the occasional sob.

"Becky?"

"Ssshhhh."

"When do they do the birching?"

"They don't tell you. Best not to worry. Now sleep." Taking Amy's hand in hers. Squeezing it tight. As the new girl watched the shadows dancing on the ceiling, until exhaustion eventually overcame her.

--

Always the same, day in, day out. The fear was overwhelming: a step out of line, and painful punishments inevitably followed.

Amy escaped retribution: concentrating, concentrating, concentrating so as not to land herself in trouble. Others were less fortunate. Susan tried to laugh off a strapping received for some perceived insult to one of the staff, but her smiles hid a much deeper gloom. Gemma fell into a dark, dark mood for a day after her transcription of the President's latest speech was deemed insufficiently neat, earning her eight sharp cuts of the cane for her 'grossly disrespectful behaviour'.

It was the sixth night after Amy's arrival when they came for Becky. Or was it the seventh? Days somehow seemed to merge under the timeless regime. It was late; the girls had been in bed for some time when the door swung open. "Officer present." The girls jumped to their bedside parade, terrified looks crossing many of their faces.

"Rebecca Drover."

Becky beginning to tremble, next to Amy. "Sir?"

"You were sentenced by the Grand Court to thirty strokes of the birch. These will now be administered. Follow me."

She tried to hold her head up high: an illusion of confidence that would be broken within minutes.

She was gone for an age. None of her dorm-mates slept. Some knew what she was going through, of course; Amy had picked up that at least two of them had already received their floggings, but none had wanted to discuss the experience in any detail. Not surprisingly, she thought. ("When will I get mine?"

she wondered. "Let it be soon: get it over with." "Please, not yet. They might forget.")

The officer's face showed no signs of sympathy when he brought Becky back. She was distraught: Amy's composed, calm, confident friend replaced by a sobbing, vulnerable girl. She lay face down in the bed, uncontrollable tears soaking the pillow. Amy stroked her hair. Placed a cooling hand on her friend's burning backside; felt her flinch. Tried to comfort, reassure as best she could, given the requirement for silence. Given the audience on the CCTV, watching their every move.

And Becky had only had thirty strokes. Amy had been sentenced to fifty.

--

Perhaps it was her inner turmoil at her friend's thrashing that led Amy to lose her concentration the following morning. Of course she should have been copying diligently: the speech that the Commissar of the General Committee had given to the West Zone's leadership was, after all, acclaimed as one of the great statements of the Party's philosophy. But across the room sat Becky; head bowed, shifting uncomfortably in her seat, her tears dropping onto her notebook. And Amy couldn't help but watch, willing her friend through the day, wanting to run over and hug her and make it better.

Willing her friend through, but failing to make progress herself with her transcription. And the supervising officer noticed, of course. Called Amy to the front. Expressed his surprise that the Commissar's work seemed so uninteresting. "Or perhaps you can recite it by heart?"

"No, sir."

And before she knew it, he had opened his desk drawer, taken out a strap and stepped down from his lectern to tower over her. "Hands!"

"But sir, you can't! This is not fair! I don't deserve…"

She felt him grab her wrists, suddenly pulling her towards the door. She struggled to stay on her feet. Out into the corridor. Still clasping her wrist: "You'll come with me. I'll show you what happens to girls who feel that they have the right to argue."

Off down corridors she hadn't seen, twisting and turning. Up a flight of whitewashed stairs. Into the unknown areas of Middlington; what must have been the highest of the towers. Into a small, windowless room, bare lest for washing facilities in the corner. The light on, as always; the camera mounted on the ceiling. Plain, unadorned walls.

Cold.

The door locked behind her, as the officer left.

Amy slumped into the corner, half annoyed at her own stupidity, half dreading the consequences.

Was that an hour that had passed? Two? Ten? Had she fallen asleep on the hard concrete? She cupped her hands, drinking the lukewarm water from the room's single tap.

Were they watching her? Would they come for her?

Another hour? Two? Five?

She cried, but crying was futile. They'd be watching her tears from their control room. Smiling. Knowing they were winning.

Another two hours? Four? Six?

--

It was the same officer who came for her, eventually, just as she'd given up hope. Led her firmly by the wrist as they retraced their steps. Led her back into the same room: the girls writing studiously, at the same tables. Brought her directly to the front of the room. Instructed her to hold out both hands. Lifted the strap high, back over his shoulder. Whipped the thick leather down hard, oh so unbelievably hard, every ounce of her being focusing onto the red stripes, as he whacked carefully, precisely, five times on each hand.

And then he sent her back to her seat, where her pen still lay on her open book. "Do continue with your work." And Amy renewed her transcription, each pen stroke cutting her to the core.

She'd been away for three days, she later discovered. Four of the girls in her dorm had left, replaced by fresh-faced newcomers. One, it seemed, had been birched on her first night:

forty strokes, still plainly visible in the morning's shower. Not that she spoke about it. Noone ever did.

--

The routine.
Still the routine. Every day, unchanging.
Amy tried to count the passing of time. Thirty days, she'd been sentenced to, as had Becky – who was still here, despite having started her sentence a few days earlier. Still here, pressing close at night, their bodies reassuring each other.
Six days left? Eight?
When would they come for her?
Another of the new girls was taken and thrashed. Shireen, in the next bed, returned from her flogging silent, and remained that way for a whole day.
"I hope they birch me before you go," whispered to Becky in their bed. I hope you'll be here, to hold me and comfort me, even if you won't be able to protect me.
And another day passed.
"Make it tonight. Please, let it be tonight."
And another day.
A hard run the following morning, outside in the rain. Down the hill, to the side of the main building, across the forest track, ferns draping their wet leaves across the girls' legs as they brushed past. Turning left by the small stream, where the dog handler stood to keep them from straying. Amy felt herself falling behind the group, but pushed on, determined not to be the last back, for who knew what penalties might be imposed on the tardy? Through the muddy clearing: back into the house. Doors shut firmly yet again.
It was only in the showers that she noticed Becky's absence. The others averted her quizzical look; silence reigned supreme. Had she slipped away, escaped through the forest? Surely they'd not taken her off into the tower?
Surely that wasn't another girl, already naked and trembling in their bed, when Amy returned to the dorm that night?
But it was. Rosie. Author of an essay that her college tutor had disliked. Had found offensive to the Committee and its

aims. Sentenced to twenty strokes and a week in Middlington. As a lesson – to her, and to her fellow students.

Rosie, needing Amy's arms as she herself had needed Becky's before.

The lights came on on the new arrival's first night. "Officer present!"; the naked parade. A female officer this time, walking through the room, making the girls lift their heads to look her in the eyes.

Stopping at the next bed. Looking at her notes. Walking on, until she stood in front of Rosie and Amy.

Her time had come...

"Rosie McArthur, you were sentenced by the Grand Court to twenty strokes of the birch. These will now be administered. Follow me." And the newcomer set off to meet her fate.

--

The longest half hour, other than your own. That wait, whilst a compatriot is being punished. Hoping that she manages to be brave. Unable to sleep; knowing the light would come back on as their victim returned. For some, the memories flooded back, of their own trip to be punished. For others, the dread fear of what might come when they took their turn, tempered by the comfort that tonight was not their night.

And Rosie hadn't taken it well: only twenty strokes, but the disciplinarians must have been on cruel form that night. She tried to smile at the other girls as she walked through their guard of honour back to her bed, but it was a pale, wan, defeated smile. Amy would have to hold her, to reassure her, as she had done with Becky. Amy the comforter.

"Amy Franklin."

What? They'd just dealt with Rosie... They only ever dealt with one girl a night. "AMY FRANKLIN."

She jolted to attention. "You were sentenced by the Grand Court to fifty strokes of the birch. These will now be administered. Follow me."

--

The officer was firm, but not unpleasant. As the dorm door closed behind them, cutting Amy off from the safe haven of her friends, she felt the cold steel clasp her wrist. "Come with me," as if she had any choice. The tiles felt chill to her feet as they paced down the corridor.

"I should daydream." Think of home, think of her sister, think of nothing. But the more she tried to think of nothing, the more she was filled with dread. This wasn't 'nothing'.

To her surprise, she found that the officer was leading her into the dining room. The dining room? The one room to which every girl must return, three times a day, after her punishment had been administered. A room that would never seem the same again, a regular reminder.

The tables had been moved to the side; a large space cleared in the middle. A triangular frame stood in the centre, made of heavy wood. Aside from the woman to whom she was handcuffed, four other officers watched her. Three tall; one short but strong-looking. She'd not expected an audience. She didn't know what she had expected, mind: everything and nothing of what was about to happen.

One of their number stepped forward, heading to the table at the rear of the room. He paused, as if making a selection, and walked towards her.

He was holding a birch.

Not one thin switch, cut from a young tree. A thick bundle of rods, bound firmly at the base. Ready to be applied.

"Amy Franklin?"

"Yes, sir."

He looked her up and down. "Tie her to the frame."

Amy's hand was uncuffed, as they led her to the position. A palm pushed her over the frame; feet pushed her legs to the outsides of its legs. More hands appeared, thick rope being tied tight around her wrists and ankles. Tight, binding her into position.

This was it.

A chorus of voices in unison behind her, as she trembled. "By order of the Committee, we, the officers of Middlington, undertake to administer the justice demanded by the State and its people, fairly, firmly and fully."

And then the stroke. Scything across her, shocking, stunning, the impact of the blow following by an agonising burning.

Oh.

My.

God.

The woman's voice, from the side of the room: "One."

One? Fifty? Fifty? One? Noooooo....

She braced herself, readying her body as best she could for the second blow. Waiting... Waiting.. Screaming as the stroke descended. Incalculable, inestimable pain.

Clear, firm: "Two."

And then the pause, making sure that she absorbed every stroke, appreciated its full severity, contemplated its successor.

"Please, no, please...." "Three".

She couldn't take it. She must take it. "Clear my mind, don't let them win, it'll be...."

"Four." A loud sob.

"...over in a few minutes. The worst is over, it's getting better, it's...."

"FUCK!"

("What have I said? Oh no. Please. No. I didn't... Forgive me. Be merciful." Aloud: "Sorry, sir.")

"We will re-administer that stroke, Miss Franklin. And add another three to the end of your birching. Might I advise you to be more circumspect in your choice of language."

"Yes, sir. Sorry...."

Owwwwwww.

"Five."

Five. Not six. Five. One stroke lost, forgotten, as if it had never happened.

Could it really be that the next strokes were harder? Was he really making her apologise for her mistake, with the awful severity of his cuts? The total mounted... six, seven, eight (astonishing – as if the previous strokes had been delivered with feathers), nine, then an excruciating tenth.

The subsequent pause was longer than ever. Footsteps echoed around the room. "Would you choose a fresh birch from the table, and take over, please, Officer?"

Amy was too tightly in position to look back, but could sense that the newcomer had taken up his place on the opposite side to his predecessor: left-handed, she supposed. The eleventh stroke, his first, certainly landed quite differently: found fresh spots on her cheeks to colour and torment.

One might assume that familiarity would breed if not contempt, then at least acceptance. That the fall of the rods would somehow become monotonous, routine.

Not so.

Each cut brought its own new agonies; each pause its dread of the next chastisement. Each cool, calm count its own recognition that the process was proceeding towards its inevitable end, an end getting closer but still unimaginably distant.

Her heaving sobs had subsided somewhat, replaced by a steady torrent of tears, but the ever-so-low fifteenth stroke quite took her breath away, before she cried for mercy and forgiveness. But neither was forthcoming: fairly, firmly and fully, they'd said, and the officers were certainly keeping their word. By the time number twenty had been announced, even Becky's caring hands would have done nothing to console her.

Twenty. Rosie had been given twenty.

But Amy had thirty to come.

Thirty. Becky had been given thirty.

In total.

And she'd been plunged into despair for days.

Officer three swapped the tallies around quickly: soon thirty down, twenty to go. His aim was hard, true, sharp – this third birch heavier than the others, if that were possible, but the strokes delivered in rapid fire. No sooner had one whack landed, than the rod descended again, the pain rising in a crescendo that left Amy spluttering, gasping for air.

Perhaps he'd been doing her a kindness? Getting the punishment over and done? Perhaps the intensity of the pain revealed that he knew he'd had the opposite effect?

"Would you choose a fresh birch from the table, and take over, please, Officer?" And the footsteps again, lighter this time, and suddenly a cool hand, a feminine hand, resting lightly on her buttocks.

The officer spoke, softly, to her colleagues: "It seems we still have some work to do."

Amy felt her move away; heard her fast steps; felt the new rods add their imprint. "Please, please, it's enough…"

"Silence." The long pause: the longest yet. "Thirty-one," and then immediately the warden danced forward, increasing the tally in the most terrible way.

Thirty-two, thirty-three, thirty-four, thirty-five. Just numbers. A counting game. Only a few, in the midst of so many. Yet each an individual stroke to be dreaded, with its own personality, its own unique stamp of authority.

Those pauses, between the application of the rods. Merciful: a respite. Cruel: drawing out the agony, allowing the fire to burn.

Thirty-six. Think of Becky, safe at home.

Thirty-seven. Tucked up in her own bed.

Thirty-eight. Loved, cared for.

Thirty-nine. Sweet saviour, forgive me, please, I'm so sorry, please….

FORTY! Finishing with a flourish, this one. Forty. Four of them done. One batch to go. Just one. I can do this. I'm nearly there…

And so the last officer stepped forward in the name of the Committee. She felt him close to her, saw him reach down towards her wrists, untie the knot, loosen the rope. He walked round her, releasing each of her bonds.

"Ten strokes to go, Miss Franklin. We like to give girls the benefit of some assistance to get through the first part of their flogging. We expect them to restrain themselves for the final few."

Silence.

"Do you understand?"

"Yes, sir."

"If you fail to hold your position, we will start the final ten anew. I encourage you to concentrate."

The experience of being flogged whilst bound to the whipping frame is scarcely imaginable. But the ties hold you down, help you to avoid concentrating on your position. Without them….?

"Forty-one."

"And we'll return to forty."

"Forty-one."

"And to forty again."

Amy clenched the wooden frame tight, although whether to clench or to relax, she knew not. All she knew was that this man was whacking her with all of his strength, and she had to summon up some reserve of courage, some sense of dignity, even when the Committee had stripped her of all that she'd thought she possessed.

"Forty-one." "Forty-two." "Forty-three." "Forty-four." In quick succession, barely time for him to count his strokes before the birch howled down once more. Testing her, as if they were willing her to fail.

A long pause. The stroke. A long pause. The next, in precisely the same spot. The next, again matching its predecessors precisely. "Forty-seven."

Becky would have been brave. Becky would have taken the final ten. Becky wouldn't want me to....

"Forty eight."

Two left. The first, a cruel blow, grazing the top of her thighs. A scream. Knuckles white. Girl still in position.

One left. Please don't let me flinch and if I just try and be brave and hold on and oh god no it can't have hurt that much hold on I must hold on please yes they're finished...

"Fifty."

And the officer was walking away, and it was over, and she could breath again, and reach up with her hand to wipe the tears. The first officer was speaking. "That completes your fifty strokes."

"Thank you, sir." Be obedient.

"All that's left is the three extras from earlier, for your foul language, and we'll be done." And he brought the rod down, the final three layered from top to bottom, ensuring their predecessors were well and truly awakened.

--

Amy remembered little of the ceremonials that took place after they'd finished, other than the signing of some official papers ("A copy of which will go to your parents") and a grave warning. "If you describe what happens in this punishment room to any other girl, both you and she will be brought here so that we can repeat the birchings that the Court prescribed for each of you."

Rosie was little comfort; Amy none for her. Neither of the birched girls slept.

The other girls looked on curiously the following morning. And moved on. No discussion. No dorm-room camaraderie. It was if nothing had happened - until she sat down. Or was tormented by a flashback. Or saw one of the officers who'd whipped her, supervising them.

It turned out that Amy had two days left: they released her early in the morning, back to the cold, dirty van that had delivered her to Middlington. The bumps and jerks on the road were more excruciating on that return journey than she could ever have predicted on her arrival.

Her family were welcoming, of course, despite the shame of the electronic billboards on every street corner proclaiming her fate: "Local girl birched: a lesson for us all."

Over time, the bruises faded; the memories did not. The birch. Middlington. Becky…

The price of privilege

Alexander Watson sipped his coffee, looking around the magnificent oak-panelled room. Yes, he thought, to himself: I could get used to this. Indeed, given time, I *will* get used to it.

Of course he'd known that the family had history. Admiral John Watson, triumphant over the Spanish fleet in the famous battle of.... what was it, again? Created Viscount Spensdale by a jubilant King, with a fine Scottish estate on which to while away his days basking in the country's gratitude.

It had been quite nice, really, to open the school history books and read about one's own flesh-and-blood. Not that the old Viscount had seemed that relevant to a family growing up in comfortable, suburban Surrey. Or, more recently, during the stresses and strains of the nine-to-five (or should that be seven-thirty-to-six-thirty) treadmill, as Alex had risen through the ranks of the company at which he worked: graduate trainee, turned 32-year-old high-flyer. No, the family's eminent history and wealth seemed a long way away as he struggled into the city each morning on the ever-less-reliable, ever-more-crowded trains.

And then that phone call. That life-changing phonecall. He remembered it clearly: how could he not? How he'd been frustrated at the interruption: that contract had to be finalised by lunchtime, and he'd specifically told Emma not to put any calls through. Her meek apologies: "They told me it was important, and that you would definitely want to take the call." Who were 'Wallace, Hamilton & Linley', anyway? They sounded like some trendy advertising agency.

They'd wanted to see him. In Edinburgh. Most insistent. About a legal matter. Something that would be of 'significant benefit and interest'.

He hadn't been able to help the flutter in his heart: what was going on? He'd never heard of these people. Untold wealth awaiting him, perhaps, he laughed to himself? A pretext, to get him to discuss some unknown offence that he'd inadvertently committed, to recover some debt that he didn't even know he'd incurred. A mistake? A joke? A con?

And in Scotland, too. They'd been so adamant; his expenses would be covered, and they really did advise him to attend at 10.30 am sharp next Monday.

It was only when their letter arrived the following morning, couriered to his office and requiring his personal signature, that he decided to go. Maybe it was the weight of the paper that convinced him, the quality oozing its importance. Perhaps the Royal crest at the bottom of the letter helped. The brochure they enclosed glowed with past and present prosperity - no flimsy, glossy marketing leaflet, this, but a leather-bound history of "Scotland's most distinguished legal advisors, founded in 1720."

Perhaps it was a sense of adventure that compelled him towards Heathrow at such an ungodly hour at the start of the following week.

Or of duty.

Suddenly, Alex snapped back into real-time.

Mortimer, the butler, was looking at him intently - as he seemed to do - disapproving, perhaps, of his master's daydreaming. Mortimer seemed to bear a permanent weight of disapproval on his shoulders, as if the new order of things did not quite fit with his ideas for Glenrossiter house. As if the young master was usurping his predecessors' place.

But, of course, he wasn't.

"Is there anything that sir would like me to do for him this morning?"

Alex glanced out of the window, looking across the perfectly-maintained lawns in the crisp spring sunshine. "I was going to walk along the river this morning, Mortimer. I haven't had a chance to explore that part of the estate yet. Could you get out my boots, please? And is there a map, by any chance?"

"Yes, sir. If I might suggest, sir, if you take the Range Rover past the farmhouse, you might park it down by the old bridge. It would save you a little walk. And then you can skirt westward along the edge of the forest for three miles, until you reach the village, then cross and walk back along the opposite riverbank."

"Thanks, Mortimer. That sounds ideal."

Deferentially, the butler added: "Sir does recall that he has an appointment at 2.30 this afternoon?"

No, Alex thought. 'Sir' did not recall. Sir didn't think he'd known anything about appointments. Today, or on any other day. Another failure in Mortimer's book, no doubt. In fact, Sir was quite looking forward to another day of leisure. Sir could get quite frustrated with his butler, if his butler wasn't careful. "Do remind me, Mortimer."

"It's explained in the papers that I left out for you on your desk yesterday, sir. If sir would like, I could go and find the documents and you could take them with you; stop and read them somewhere on your stroll?"

"But I don't want to..." Alex thought to himself. Yet something in the older man's voice made him think that this meeting, whatever it might be, wasn't optional. Damn it, he thought: meetings, paperwork were for my former life. He folded his crisp white napkin, yawned, and set off to his bedroom suite, still grumbling silently to himself. Well, he thought, whatever this appointment is, it had better be important.

--

"I'm so ashamed."

"Mother, please..."

"My own daughter. Suspended from school. And the first girl sent up to his new lordship."

"Please..."

"You've brought shame on our household, Jennifer Elizabeth. Shame..."

As if this helped. When she needed support. Hugs. Reassurance. Love, to quell her fear.

She was trying to look brave, of course. Nonchalant. But since her sentence had been pronounced, she'd thought of nothing else. Well you wouldn't, would you?

Why her? Why not Libby, or Beth, or Elise? They'd helped. They'd urged her on. Why had it had to be her?

Her mother's complaints continued, rising in a crescendo of allegations and grievances.

And she turned, and ran upstairs, slamming her bedroom door shut and flinging herself face down on her bed, not ashamed to sob.

--

A glorious morning, Alex thought, as he breathed in the crisp, clean air - so far from London with all its pollution. He still had to pinch himself to believe this was true.

Who would have thought: his rich great-uncle - well, to be precise, not even a great-uncle: the relationship was far more indirect than that, but a bloodline, nonetheless. And not even just rich. A peer of the realm; the most recent Viscount Spensdale, no less, the descendant of the old Admiral whose whiskery face had peered out from the history books.

The 'late' Viscount Spensdale, to be precise. The late, childless Viscount Spensdale, the presumed last of the line. Whose distinguished Edinburgh lawyers had engaged an expert genealogist in one last attempt to trace any distant descendants who could inherit the title and estate, and who had hence ended up some months later on the other end of Alex's phone line.

Well, he thought, he was here now. No jokers had emerged to reveal their pranks. No hidden reality-TV cameras had exposed their trickery. Thirty-two years old, that long commute to the office to earn the money to pay the monthly rent a thing of the past. He felt like he'd retired early. Very early.

That, in itself, would be a challenge - would he get bored? Alex had no interest in the minutiae of running a large estate like Glenrossiter - and anyway, the Estate Manager seemed more than competent. And meanwhile, the canny investment decisions of decades of past Viscounts meant that the most complex monetary decision he would ever need to make was whether to scan the share prices in the Financial Times before or after breakfast.

He paused, noticing a crop of rocks at the side of the river, and perched himself comfortably on them. He would have taken off his boots and socks and dangled his feet in the water, had he not dipped his hands in earlier and felt the chill edge from the still-melting snows of the mountains that fringed the eastern edge of the estate.

This is the life, he thought happily. I could get used to this, he thought again. I am getting used to this, even two weeks in. He smiled, thinking about the coming weekend; his friends arriving to stay, the chauffeur meeting them at the airport. No doubt curious, envious - but friends, still, their friendships - he so hoped - unaffected by his good fortune. Mark and Susie, Matthew and Kirsty, Peter, Amber, Caitlin, Millie.

Especially Millie. Things had just started to... to be clearer, when all of this had happened. Deep, confused thoughts had started to crystallise for both of them; their goodnight hugs had started to grow more tender; their confidences in each other more frank. And then all of this... He looked around, pride and astonishment still mixing in equal proportions as he took in the views, smelt the fresh grass, watched as a bird of prey - eagle, hawk? - flew overhead.

From his small rucksack, he extracted the purple folder that Mortimer had retrieved from the office. He smiled, at the thought of his study; its jumble of papers and books, a whole family history of a family he hadn't known, just waiting to be discovered. And he started to read...

--

From the Headmistress
Glenrossiter Grammar School for Girls.

My Lord,

Might I start by welcoming you to Glenrossiter. We hope that you will find yourself at home here.

Please also accept my sincere condolences on the passing of the late Viscount Spensdale. His lordship was a dear friend to the Grammar School over the years and we share your sadness.

You may not yet be aware that under our school's charter, you now hold the legal position of Visiting Governor. This gives you the right to appoint or dismiss members of the school's governing body, and ultimate authority over decisions relating to the school. Your post is enshrined in legal statutes, and we do hope that we will be able to count on your active support.

As he became less able to participate in public life, the late Viscount Spensdale delegated these authorities to Sir Thomas Brownrigg. However, the legal paperwork that was signed at the time made it clear that his responsibilities would revert automatically to any future holder of the Viscount's title.

Whilst I look forward to welcoming you more formally in due course, and to discussing your role in more detail, there is one area in which I need to ask for your immediate support. One of the roles of Visiting Governor is to administer discipline in cases of serious breaches of the school's rules. You might recall that corporal punishment is outlawed in United Kingdom schools as a result of legislation in the 1980s. However, a legal anomaly dating from the time of the original creation of the viscountcy meant that our statutes made us exempt from this legislation under Scottish law. We do, therefore, somewhat unusually, retain the cane as a measure of last resort for the most grave misdemeanours.

It is most unfortunate that one of our senior girls committed an offence last week which I deem worthy of such a punishment, when Jennifer Murray was found to have stolen the question paper for a forthcoming examination from the staff common room. Having checked with your staff, I understand that 2.30 pm on Wednesday would be a convenient time for you to deal with Miss Murray, and I have therefore instructed her to report to you to be disciplined at that time. She has also been suspended for one week.

Might I conclude by saying once again how pleased we are to have you with us in Glenrossiter, and offering you any assistance that may help as you settle in.

Yours truly,

Georgina Sinclair (Miss).

--

Alex let out a whistle of astonishment, and laid the letter down on the rock beside him. His mind buzzed with information. Wow... I mean, good grief. But... I'd expected some official duties. But this? Well, Miss (note the emphasis on the Miss) Sinclair seemed a fair character. What a letter. And as for Jennifer... what was her name again? (he picked up the paper and checked)... Jennifer Murray. Well, poor girl. Actually, not poor girl, if she'd been stealing.

The young peer stood up, pushing the papers into his bag and turned back towards the house. Did he really have to do this? Cane this girl? Where would he get a cane, anyway? And how did one cane a girl, for that matter? He cast his mind back to the school stories he'd read in his childhood: Tom Brown, of course. The Jennings books. Roald Dahl. Bend her over and give her six of the best, he assumed. But that was easier to say in theory than to do in practice, and he certainly didn't want to make a fool of himself.

He wandered back, trying to think about other things: the plans for his friends' visit; how much he'd like to explore and catalogue the huge, disorganised library at Glenrossiter. But again and again he found himself drawn back, half horrified and half fascinated, to his impending meeting with young Miss Murray.

--

She showered, trying to escape her fears under the hot running water.

He sat down for lunch, under Mortimer's watchful gaze.

She dressed, carefully, her freshly-laundered uniform so neatly ironed by her mother.

He beckoned the butler to him, and asked about the school.

She muttered under her breath: "I hate that place. I can't wait to escape, to get to university."

He enquired about the school's traditions, and was assured that the late Viscount Spensdale had taken his traditional responsibilities most seriously.

She peered into the mirror, brushing her hair for slightly longer than was really necessary, trying to imagine what it might be like. Then trying to forget her imaginings.

He wondered about Jennifer Murray. How must she be feeling at this moment, knowing she was due to be whacked?

She wondered about the new viscount. Young, she heard. From England. What would he be feeling at this moment? Would he be thinking about her?

He was informed by Mortimer that his cane had been placed next to the fireplace in the drawing room.

She wondered, nervously, how many strokes she would get.

He learnt that his old lordship used to claim that eight of the best, on the bare backside, was necessary to deal with the mischief-makers. Listened to the protocol, understood what was expected of him.

She wished she had someone to talk to, someone who could give her a hug.

He ate his lunch slowly, unable to enjoy the food.

She went downstairs, past her mother, leaving her unwanted lunch untouched.

He wished he didn't have to do this.

She wished he didn't have to do this.

He pushed his plate away, and headed for the drawing room.

She closed the front door behind her, and headed for the path that lead through the forest to the great estate.

And he looked at his watch...

... as she realised it was five past two, and started to hurry.

--

He studied the girl, taking in her crisp, smart uniform, her red badge standing out against the black blazer. Tie neatly fastened. Tartan skirt - a kilt, almost. And he watched her tremble, and wondered.

Wondered what she must be feeling, and wondered about her offence.

"It must be Jennifer." A face to the name; the words on the letter replaced by living, breathing (and, he dared to think, attractive) flesh. Two dimensions turned into three as his paper responsibilities suddenly took on a very real form.

"Yes, sir." She took in her surroundings: the high ceiling, the paintings. The smell of fresh lilies. Oh, the very comfort of the room. A room she'd love to live in, curl up in, be warm in. Not...

He beckoned to the chair. "Take a seat, Jennifer. Do they call you Jennifer, by the way? Or Jenny?"

"Jenny, Lord Spensdale." She looked at him nervously, folding her hands on her lap as she sank into the armchair. He wasn't what she'd imagined a Lord would look like; in fact, he looked quite nice. Sounded friendly, even, not like that horrible butler who'd shown her in, grinning maliciously.

Alex sat down opposite her, leaning forward. "So what year are you in at the School, Jenny?"

"I'm in my final year, sir. Going to university in the autumn. "

"Very good. What do you want to study?"

"Law, sir. At St. Andrew's. If I get straight 'A' grades in my exams, that is."

"You must be bright, then?" He'd known a girl from St. Andrew's, years back. Old and distinguished - the university, that is. Unlike Sophie, who'd been young and most adventurous.

Jenny blushed. "Yes, sir, I suppose so. I get good grades, and the interview went well." This was sounding like a careers discussion; she could almost let herself forget why she was here. Almost.

"So you're bright, you're smart. What on earth brings you here?"

She gulped. What brought her here? Recklessness. A dare. A desire to prove herself to the other girls. "Well, sir, we were… I… was… trying to impress some of the others."

He looked at her quizzically. "Impress them?"

"Yes, sir. Well, we were talking. Me and some… friends. About our mock exams - we've got Highers next term, so we're sitting practice papers in two weeks' time. And about how much easier it would be to revise if they gave us the papers in advance…" Her voice trailed off, as she looked down at the carpet.

"Go on."

"Well, sir, it's a long story. But I nipped into the common room one evening, after the teachers had all gone home, and managed to find the History paper."

"I see. Not a good idea."

"No, sir." No, sir, not a good idea at all. Not a good idea if you were the sort of girl who didn't do that kind of thing. Not a good idea in any circumstances, in fact. Even if you did so want to be popular with the other girls; to be liked; to be in with the in-crowd.

He stood up, and her eyes followed him as he walked over to the fireplace. "I'm somewhat surprised at you, given that you want to be a lawyer. One might expect rather more responsible behaviour." He picked up the stick, watching her eyes widen, and continued. "So now you're here, and since I am apparently your 'Visiting Governor', I have to give you the cane."

She bit her lip, then pleaded. Well, you would, wouldn't you? You would try and make this man - with his obvious kindly side underneath the steely determination - you would try and make him relent. But she knew her petitions were futile, even as they slipped out of her mouth: "You don't have to, sir. Please. I know I shouldn't have done it."

And she did know. He could tell. But he couldn't not proceed. Couldn't break the trust that the school, the community, obviously placed in him. Let them down. He beckoned her to her feet: "I'm afraid I don't have a choice, Jenny. Have you been caned before?"

"Never, sir." Never. Never would a girl like her expect to find herself here. Never.

Never, ever would a girl like her expect to feel the wooden back of a tall wooden chair against her skin, as she bent over on tiptoes, exposed, her shoes and socks on the floor, her blazer, skirt and knickers folded neatly on the table.

To hear him award her eight strokes. Eight! To feel him press the stick against her, cold and straight, and draw it back. To experience that pause before it landed, that final moment: part wait, part anticipation, part relief, but mainly sheer terror - knowing that any moment now she would turn into a whipped girl.

Never, either, would he have imagined himself disciplining a semi-naked schoolgirl. But Alex was beginning to understand that with the privilege, the estate, the title and the undreamt-of wealth, came responsibility. Expectation.

Authority.

The sound of the descending rod against her buttocks was softer than he'd imagined when he'd thwacked the cushions earlier. Softer, sharper. Yet the cushions hadn't cried out, anguished and pitiful; the cushions hadn't striped, angry and red. The cushions hadn't squirmed.

He watched her closely, as he proceeded with the punishment, concentrating on making the strokes land precisely against their target. She was braver than he would have thought possible, yet at the same time more vulnerable, more fragile as she writhed under the blows.

Alex looked up at the portraits on the wall, and imagined his distinguished predecessors meting out similar thrashings. Imagined the other girls who must have bent over chairs and tables in this very room, receiving their correction. Well, he thought: those who'd been before - those Spensdales of old: he wouldn't let them down. And he tightened his grip on the cane, and lifted it higher, and cut it down still harder. Four... five...

By the sixth stroke, the girl's reaction was becoming more even - no longer cries of anguish at each terrible blow, but a steady catching of breath a whimpering, shoulders heaving. Was this the price she'd had to pay - to be Jenny the popular, Jenny the brave, Jenny the liked?

And then, almost before the punishment had begun, yet a changed lifetime afterwards, the final two sharp blows had been dispensed. He was telling her to stand up, to dress, turning away so that she could hang onto those strands of modesty that remained. She pulled on the clothes quickly, anxiously. It wasn't smart, impeccably-turned out Jennifer now; gone was the tidiness, along with the bravado. It was just small, sobbing, sorry Jenny. In need of a hug.

A hug which wouldn't, couldn't come from the new Viscount, no matter how sad and pitiful the poor girl looked. Alex waited for her, watched her, let her compose herself as best she could, then pressed the bell on the side-table. Before the echoes of its chimes had even subsided, the door swung open, and Mortimer appeared. (Had he been listening to the punishment, Alex later wondered? Listening, assessing, judging. Enjoying?)

"Is his Lordship finished with the girl?"

He looked at her. "I do hope so. Let us agree that our next meeting will be in more fortuitous circumstances, Miss Murray."

"Yes, sir. Sorry, sir. Please don't think badly of me, sir..."

Her apologies were interrupted. "Out of here, at the double," Mortimer commanded. "Shall I bring you a cup of tea, sir, once I've shown the girl out?"

"Yes, Mortimer, that would be kind." And Alex turned, and walked back across the room, throwing himself back into the comfort of an armchair and picking up the copy of The Field, as the girl disappeared.

--

That evening, the Reverend Michael Donaldson proved to be great company for dinner at the great house. Witty, entertaining and learned.

Jenny's dining table experience was of a rather different nature. Her mother, still belligerent, ordered her to her room as soon as she reached home. Sent her to bed, like a naughty little girl. Which in some ways, she supposed, wasn't too far from the truth.

And there she stayed, body and pride equally wounded, until her father slammed shut the front door on his return from work, and yelled for her to join them in the dining room.

She knew she'd let herself down.

She knew she'd embarrassed her parents.

She knew she'd put her chances of a university place at risk, and that she was fortunate that the school hadn't told St. Andrew's.

She knew she'd brought shame on the family.

She knew she'd deserved to be caned, to be punished, to be taught an unforgettable lesson, to be made an example of by the school.

She knew her parents were angry.

She knew that they wanted her to succeed.

She knew, even, despite the shouting, that they loved her dearly.

And she knew then, before her father even said the words, before he pointed to the table, even before he reached for the buckle of his sturdy leather belt, that whilst the school's discipline had already been administered, her debt to her family had not yet been repaid.

Someone to care

"This really is most disappointing, Samantha. I'm afraid to say that we're going to have to deal with this later, in my study."

Had he really said that, as he'd looked up from the small, black leather-bound notebook, eyebrows raised?

Lauren's hands trembled as she picked up the plates for the next table. "Table 12. One fillet steak, medium-rare. One sea bass."

Had he known that she was standing there, that she'd inevitably overhear?

Had that been the very point?

--

She always let herself concoct little stories about the patrons she was serving. That couple over there: the French baron and his daughter, fresh from their shopping trip to Harrods. The elderly gentlemen in his usual Tuesday lunchtime table in the corner: Professor Sir Maximus Smythe, Nobel Prize winner back in '67. The young lady in the corner, toying with the salad – a courtesan, awaiting the call that would summon her to the private room in the gentlemen's club just round the corner...

Well, it certainly made the time pass quicker, and since she'd been a little girl, her fantasies had always seemed more colourful than real life. Even here, in London. London! Especially here. She still had to pinch herself as she strolled the streets, as if an actor on the set of some non-stop movie – even if the competing realities of a tough deadline for her Masters thesis and the need to earn money in this exorbitantly expensive city meant that life was often more grind than glitz.

She'd been lucky to get a job in Pampas, mind: such exhilarating fun to work in one of the city's more upmarket restaurants. Serving fine Argentinian beef to well-to-do customers had to beat frothing milk for the long trail of impatient customers in the Starbucks where she'd first worked after arriving. That said, even Starbucks had seemed cool: Belinda's Coffee House was about as glamorous as it got back home.

Home. A distant place – across the ocean. (Could you believe it? I've crossed an ocean. Me, from the small farm in the small town that noone's ever heard of). Home. A distant memory. (How often did they think about her? How often she missed the comfort, the security of her family sometime).

She wasn't lonely, as such. How could she be? So much to do, so much to explore, in those precious moments when work, academic or paid, didn't dominate her every minute. She'd trade: twenty minutes in the National Gallery for twenty minutes less in front of the TV. A half-hour of the British Museum for a half-hour in bed. (Particularly given that bed wasn't exactly an exciting place: perhaps she should have gone to Italy if she'd wanted to find Romeo?).

No, not lonely. Just... At school, it'd been different: a half-step out of line, and a teacher would notice, would scold, would punish – just as, more often, they'd praise when she did well. At home, too: even when Daddy called her, or Casey, or them both into his study, she knew that it was because he loved them and wanted them to do well. Even if his lectures hurt far more than the agonies of his thick, doubled-up belt.

Same at university, for her first degree: tutors who checked for essays, noted missed classes, especially for one of their brightest students. But here? "Please submit your thesis by 1 June, Miss Taylor. Do drop by if you need anything in the meantime." (You've paid your money. Do we really care beyond that?)

Oh, how she longed for someone to take an interest. To notice that the today's *fifty* minutes in the museum had included twenty that should have been spent in the library. To worry that last night's 34,769 words seemed a long way from the 60,000 that were due at the end of the academic year.

To check the cupboard, and care that the dried fruit had been replaced by chocolate biscuits, and that the bathroom scales were buried under a pile of unwashed laundry. To run a finger through the dust. To raise an eyebrow, and comment that "This really is disappointing, Lauren."

--

The empty table to their right: the napkins aren't quite straight.

("So do you have an explanation, Samantha?" "No, sir. I mean, I've been trying, but...")

Their wine: his glass needs refilling. "Thank you, young lady."

("I really meant to, but...", then silence and blushes as their waitress drew near. "Then you leave me little choice but to deal with you later...").

That group sitting behind them. The American oil tycoon, with his mistress? "Another bottle of wine, maybe?" "That'd be just great: thanks."

("Now, Alison. I'd like to read your notebook, please." "Yes, sir...")

Their dinner plates to clear: "Was everything to your satisfaction?" "Excellent, as ever."

("You seem to have been trying extremely hard since our last little discussion." "I really wanted to do better this time, sir...")

Dessert? Coffee? "No thank you. I'm afraid we have some matters to deal with before the afternoon is out."

(Samantha, unable to lift her eyes from her lap. "Alison, I think you might want to go back to the library, don't you? Your friend can meet you there once we've finished.")

Thank you's, and compliments to the chef. "Hope to see you soon, sir." A penetrating glance: blue eyes, looking straight into hers, reading her secrets. "Indeed. That would be my pleasure."

(His *pleasure*?)

And then they were gone.

(Be brave, Samantha. I'm thinking of you...)

--

"Lauren..." Fernando, the ever-so-gorgeous Maitre D', caught her arm as she passed, rushing to return a precariously balanced pile of plates to the kitchen. Busy, busy, busy.

"Hiya."

"You seem to have an admirer, sweetie."

"Pardon?" (Now if it was Fernando himself...)

"The gentleman who's just arrived on table 32 has specifically asked whether you might look after him today. He told me you did a very good job when he was here a couple of lunchtimes ago."

Heart-stopping. Then a shudder. A gentleman? *That* gentleman? The one she'd been thinking about, her mind drifting every few hours to the thoughts of him, and to Samantha, and to her own behaviour and hopes, and fears?

Pluck up the courage. You probably imagined it all. It won't be him.

It was. He was wearing a red tie today. Immaculately-pressed white shirt; cufflinks, of course, peeking out from beneath his dark suit. He smiled as she approached.

He's just another guest, nothing different. Don't be silly. Don't make a fool of yourself. Don't get hurt.

"Good afternoon, sir. Welcome back to Pampas."

He smiled, as if happy to see her. "How very pleasant to see you again. Lauren, isn't it?"

"Yes, sir." (How had he found *that* out?). "A drink, to start with?"

"I shall have a glass of my usual red, please."

Panic: his usual? The look of confusion must have been plain, for he questioned her: "You do remember, I hope? It was only two lunchtimes ago."

"I'm sorry, sir. A Malbec, wasn't it?" How could he do this? Throw her off her guard, cut through the façade of her composure, almost with his first sentence?

"Luigi Bosca Gala 2. I believe it was the 2003?"

"Of course, sir." Damn, damn, damn. She wanted to make a good impression: Lauren the professional - calm, collected, confident, competent. Not Lauren the little girl, pretending to be a wonderful waitress at home in these swanky surroundings.

She returned as quickly as she could. It was only as she leant over to pour the deep red wine into the glass that she happened to glance at the table, and notice. A small, black leather-bound notebook sat on the crisp tablecloth. And yet there were no girls with him for lunch today.

--

To get through his meal unnoticed. Serve him perfectly. Watch him sign the bill, proffer a generous tip (as he had done last time). Thank him, offer him his coat, show him to the door. Watch him disappear into the street.

Disappear, leaving her alone.

But the notebook. Just like Samantha's. Alison's. (Other girls'?). There on the table: looking at her. An invitation: RSVP? Could she? Did she dare?

His accent suggested a good education, a good life: prosperity, a natural air of command. Officer class, for sure. His comments carefully measured: polite, friendly, yet demanding attention, compliance. Requiring and expecting only the highest standards. She served him as if he were a king, wanting him to notice how well she worked, to forget her initial slip about the wine.

And soon he was sipping his coffee, and asking for the bill, and drawing crisp notes from his wallet.

"Thank you, Lauren. It's a delight to be looked after by such a charming young lady."

"You're very kind, sir."

"You remind me of some of my friends. You might remember the young ladies who dined with me on Tuesday?"

"Yes, sir. They seemed very... pleasant." And she reminded him of them? Stay calm, Lauren, stay calm.

"Indeed. I thought you would remember them. After all, you did seem to listen in to our conversation throughout lunch..."

"But sir..."

"... and so I think you understand that I offer them a little... moral support... to help them to cope with London life."

"Yes, sir." Blushing deeply. Squirming. From embarrassment, and...

He picked up the small tray from the table, with the bill and his payment. And then picked up the black leather notebook, and placed it on top, handing it to her.

"I think you might find this useful. I mean, I may be mistaken, but I'm usually not." And with that he stood, and smiled, and thanked her for looking after him. Hands trembling, she led him towards the door; offered him his coat. Watched him disappear into the street.

--

The address had been printed on the card within the notebook. She'd walked there straight after lunch, naturally. A tall house, on a beautiful square, in what she knew to be one of the best areas of the city.

Walked there, walked past, walked back past, walked back again. And then fled, running, to the tube, and to her flat, and to the safety of the bedroom. Where she'd opened the letter that had been folded within the notebook, and allowed herself to read. Neat handwriting, blue ink:

"Dear Lauren,

I could not help but notice your curiosity at my conversation with my friends on Tuesday.

Sometimes, successful young women in a strange city need a little help to focus on doing the right things, in the right way. Sometimes, they turn to me for assistance, to help to monitor their progress.

They use a notebook to record their behaviour, and present it to me for regular review. And they learn to accept the consequences should their conduct fall short of my, and their, high standards.

I do hope that you are enjoying life in our city, and that you are completely content. Should, however, you require additional support, you now have my notebook – and my address. I shall be at home tomorrow, Friday, at 4 pm

With all best wishes,

Henry Settington"

--

Which was why she'd been up all night, writing in the notebook.

Which was why she'd changed, after work (so hard to concentrate on serving the lunchtime diners) into her smart suit and nicest blouse. ("Going for an interview?" Fernando had asked. "Not deserting us, sweetie?")

Which was why she'd arrived in the square twenty minutes before four, to be sure not to be late. Walked around the block three, four times, so as not to be observed. Checked her watch. Rechecked it, two minutes later. One minute later. Fifteen seconds later.

Which was why she'd stopped as she stepped onto the grand marble doorstep; almost turned to run.

Which was why she'd pressed the bell, and taken a deep breath.

The confusion that crossed her face when another man opened the door must have been plain, for he quickly reassured: "Miss Lauren, I presume? Sir Henry is expecting you. Do come in. I'm, William, his butler"

A butler? He has a butler?

Sir Henry?

He was *expecting* me?

Lauren looked around her: she's spent enough time in museums and galleries to recognise that this place, were it ever to open to the public, would draw in the crowds in their thousands.

"Please, come this way. Sir Henry has a visitor at the moment, but he should be free very shortly. Would you mind waiting for a few moments in the drawing room, Miss Lauren? Tea while you wait? Earl Grey to your liking? Lemon?"

She laid her notebook on the table, and sank into the deep, green armchair, before remembering why she was here and sitting back up, straight. Wouldn't do to slouch, would it?

The butler (me? in a house with a butler?) reappeared at her elbow, offering to pour her drink into the fine china cup through the fine, silver tea strainer. A dog appeared, too: a spaniel of some type, tail wagging, keen to meet his master's new acquaintance. William led him off; she was left alone, watched only by the stern gazes from the portraits lining the walls.

I want to run away…

It'd be rude to run away now…

I don't want to run away…

And then she heard the crack, and the squeal, through the door at the end of the room. And another. And she realised that she wasn't the only girl seeing Sir Henry this afternoon.

A… girl… is… being… punished. There, on the other side of that door.

It sounds like it hurts.

A lot.

And I am sitting here.

And, in a few moments, I'll be in there.

And he won't like everything in my notebook. I'm ashamed of some of the things in my notebook. He'll punish me for some of the things in my notebook.

I want to run away…

It'd be rude to run away now…

I don't want to run away…

And it was a good thing she hadn't, for within moments the door at the end of the room flew open, and Sir Henry appeared, followed by Alison, wiping away tears.

He smiled warmly at her. "How lovely to see you, Lauren. I believe that you met Alison earlier in the week, albeit in rather different circumstances."

They nodded, murmured hellos, the new girl to her new friend. Her *punished* friend – a mirror, reflecting Lauren-in-half-an-hour?

"I'm afraid that Alison has just been learning a little lesson: what happens to girls who are less than honest in what they write into their notebooks. Haven't you?"

Sob. "Yes, sir." Sob.

"But that's forgiven now, and she won't do it again. Will you, Alison." The final phrase seemed more of a statement than a question, but she answered nonetheless: "No, sir."

Suddenly, from behind Lauren – how long had he been there? – came William's voice. "Would you like me to show you out, Miss Alison?"

"Thank you, William, that would be kind." The sentence eloquent; its intonation less fluent from the punished girl. She turned to Sir Henry: "Thank you, sir. I shall see you next week." And she leant forward to Lauren, whispering: "He's a wonderful man. Good luck"

And with that, she and the butler were gone, and Lauren was being ushered into the next room, and the door was closing behind them, and she and the gentleman were alone.

--

An enclosed room - a library, of sorts: books lining the walls, an imposing leather-topped desk straight ahead. Globes decorating the surfaces: old globes, museum-quality globes. Light peering in from windows high up – presumably, to avoid damaging the precious volumes on the shelves.

He sat behind the desk; made her stand in front of it.

"Might I have your notebook, Lauren?"

"Yes, sir." She trembled as she passed her fate willingly into his hands.

He looked up, smiling. A friendly smile: surprisingly warm. And then he looked serious once more. "You understand why you are here, and what is likely to transpire between us?"

She nodded. Oh, how she understood. How she needed what she understood.

"I can't hear you, young lady."

"Yes, sir. I understand."

"Then would you care to tell me precisely what you understand."

I understand that Daddy is far away, across the ocean. I understand that my teachers don't care. I understand the look on Samantha and Alison's faces. I understand the need for someone to take an interest. Gulp: "I understand that you will check my behaviour, sir, and punish me if I disappoint."

"And is that what you want?"

She bit her lip, before answering quietly. "Yes, sir. Yes please, sir."

"Good girl. Now, do take a seat."

She sat before him, watching as he toyed with the notebook. "What will I find when I read what you have written, Lauren?"

Hurried, garbled: she hadn't expected him to ask, only to read. "That I try to be good sir, I really do, but sometimes things just happen and London's so amazing and there's so much to do and..."

"I see. And I understand, really I do. I never cease to be fascinated by the city and its endless quirks and novelties. Yet one's time for fascination must be limited by one's duties, I always feel."

"Yes, sir."

"And your notebook: an honest account? The truth and the whole truth?"

"Of course, sir."

"You see, young Alison told me on Tuesday that she'd dealt with various things that needed resolving. Yet a couple of phone calls from William confirmed my suspicion that she may have been somewhat economical with her account. He needed to check whether his niece still had any library books outstanding, that sort of thing, and they were only too happy to give him the information. And it's not the outstanding library books that really mattered, or the failed promise to return them: it was the dishonesty in telling me that she had done so when she had not."

And that was why she'd emerged, tear-stained from this very room. (How had he punished her? How would she herself be dealt with?) "I'll always be honest, sir, in everything I write."

"Good girl. Honest with yourself: never forget that that's even more important than being honest with me." And with that he fell into silence, and opened the notebook, and started to read.

A raised eyebrow.

A smile, as if of recognition.

A frown.

And then a fountain pen (the one with which he had written his letter to her?) picked up: a note made on the crested paper before him. Another scribble followed, a page or so later. And that was when she knew for sure that he was going to punish her that afternoon: that the contents of her book were sufficient to condemn her.

Did it take him five minutes, twenty, more, to read? She hardly knew: time stood still in their hidden capsule – just the two of them, locked away, analysing her behaviour. Sir Henry, writing his little notes on grave matters on the paper on the desk; weighing the consequences.

He closed the book, and moved the papers on his desk to one side. He must have read what she'd written about meeting him and the girls at lunch. About her heart fluttering when he returned – a gentleman coming back to claim his new girl?

"Would you stand, please, Lauren?"

He smiled again: no harshness here. She felt reassured, comforted. Cared for. "You are a good, honest, decent girl, aren't you?"

"I try to be, sir."

"I confess to being quite taken with the thought that you have put into your account. Most impressive."

"Thank you, sir."

"And yet there are some issues within it that require further discussion, are there not?"

And at last someone was going to discuss them with her. "There are, sir."

"Would you care to tell me what you think they might be?"

Plead guilty for me. Tell me what you did. Then I'll pass sentence. "I don't always work as hard as I might, sir. I don't always keep to my promises. I don't look after my flat. I... I tell everyone I'm doing fine, but there's noone who really listens, so I kind of try and get away with it."

He had taken off his jacket and walked behind her as she spoke, and laid a gentle hand on her shoulder. "Which is why I'm here to listen. And to read. And to help."

"Yes, sir."

He spoke softly, leaning in close. "In our future meetings, each of the many things you describe would individually merit a lengthy discussion."

"Yes, sir. I understand." Why did 'discussion' come with such foreboding undertones?

"But this afternoon, on our first meeting, I intend to wipe your slate clean. So that I may help you to start afresh, and focus on the things that really matter, I'd like you to lift your skirt and bend over my desk."

Funny how a deep sense of calm can turn to terror, without pausing for breath at curiosity en route. So this was it? "I'm so sorry, sir," she apologised as she leant forward

"In England, we've long used the cane to punish and to discipline, and I am a firm believer in applying traditional methods where they work so effectively."

"Yes, sir." The cane? Now. Here? Her?

"You will count the strokes as I administer them. There'll be eight in all. And as you take your caning bravely, I'd like you to contemplate your future good conduct."

"Yes, sir," and then she felt her knickers being lowered. Bare, to be punished. As she needed to be. As she dreaded.

Is this really happening?

Please don't let it hurt too much.

I want to run away...

I need, so need, to stay here...

Suddenly - the pain, indescribable. Daddy's belt had never cut like this, never seared in such anger. But it had never had so many months of misconduct to address.

A pause, as the throbbing intensified across the cane's cruel stripe. "I thought I asked you to count?"

"One, sir. I'm sorry, I…"

One, and then two, and then three, and then the numbers were being spoken by pure reflex, any ability to articulate coherently lost as the pain welled and the sense of being punished grew. Fighting back tears. Giving way to them. Feeling them trickle down her cheeks and drop, drop, drop onto the desk below.

It hurt. Oh, how it hurt. Oh, how bad she must have been.

And, as he finished, she knew how much she needed it to hurt, to correct, to show her that someone cared.

A voice: distant, behind her. His voice, drawing her back into the world. "Would you adjust your clothing, please, and then come over here." She reached back, drew up her knickers, felt her swollen, hot backside.

Moments later, he had beckoned her to him and drawn her into his arms. He let her tears soak his shoulder; told her how privileged he felt to be able to help her. Let her know how brave she had been. (Was I? Really?).

She dried her face, and thanked him. "I'm sorry that I've done all these things so badly, sir, but I'm going to try much harder now."

"That's wonderful to hear, my dear. It would give me great joy to see you happier and still more successful."

Sir Henry walked back around his desk, and drew a volume from the drawer. He flicked through the pages: "It seems that I am seeing Samantha and Alison for lunch on Monday week. Rules, in Covent Garden. Do you know it?"

"No, sir."

"Then if you're able to plan your shifts and your academic work accordingly, might I have the pleasure of introducing you to one of my favourite establishments? With your notebook updated, of course. Midday sharp, for lunch – and then as long as it takes thereafter. Unless you think that our discussion this afternoon has sufficed?"

She smiled at him, through the pain. "Our discussion has been extremely helpful, sir, and I'd be very grateful to you if you would continue to help me."

"It will be my pleasure, Lauren."

And with that, he led her the library door, opening it to reveal William standing directly outside ready to show her back out to start her new London life, with her new resolutions. And with someone to care.

About the author

Abel is one of the world's foremost writers of spanking erotica. His website, "Abel's Spanking Stories", was launched in 1999 and is one of the longest-standing and most popular sites of its type.

His early stories were selected to feature in the prestigious "Laura's Spanking Corner" and have appeared in print in magazines such as Kane. He won the first major writing competition hosted by the Spanking Online website.

With his wife Haron, Abel also co-authors "The Spanking Writers" blog, updated daily since April 2006. Anthologies of the "best of" the blog are available from Amazon and other book retailers.

Abel lives in England, where he is an active member of the spanking community.

Visit the author at
www.spankingwriters.com

www.ingramcontent.com/pod-product-compliance
Ingram Content Group UK Ltd.
Pitfield, Milton Keynes, MK11 3LW, UK
UKHW041438180426
11947UKWH00007B/507